REAL
CALM

Handle stress and take
back control

PSYCHOLOGIES
MAGAZINE

This edition first published 2017
© 2017 Kelsey Publishing Ltd

Registered office
John Wiley and Sons Ltd, The Atrium, Southern Gate, Chichester, West Sussex, PO19 8SQ, United Kingdom

For details of our global editorial offices, for customer services and for information about how to apply for permission to reuse the copyright material in this book please see our website at www.wiley.com.

Wiley publishes in a variety of print and electronic formats and by print-on-demand. Some material included with standard print versions of this book may not be included in e-books or in print-on-demand. If this book refers to media such as a CD or DVD that is not included in the version you purchased, you may download this material at http://booksupport.wiley.com. For more information about Wiley products, visit www.wiley.com.

Designations used by companies to distinguish their products are often claimed as trademarks. All brand names and product names used in this book and on its cover are trade names, service marks, trademark or registered trademarks of their respective owners. The publisher and the book are not associated with any product or vendor mentioned in this book. None of the companies referenced within the book have endorsed the book.

Limit of Liability/Disclaimer of Warranty: While the publisher and author have used their best efforts in preparing this book, they make no representations or warranties with the respect to the accuracy or completeness of the contents of this book and specifically disclaim any implied warranties of merchantability or fitness for a particular purpose. It is sold on the understanding that the publisher is not engaged in rendering professional services and neither the publisher nor the author shall be liable for damages arising herefrom. If professional advice or other expert assistance is required, the services of a competent professional should be sought.

Library of Congress Cataloging-in-Publication Data is available

A catalogue record for this book is available from the British Library.

ISBN 978-0-857-08666-2 (pbk)
ISBN 978-0-857-08667-9 (ebk)   ISBN 978-0-857-08668-6 (ebk)

Cover design: Wiley

Set in 9.5/13pt ITC Franklin Gothic Std by Aptara

Printed in Great Britain by TJ International Ltd, Padstow, Cornwall, UK

CONTENTS

FOREWORD   by Suzy Greaves, Editor, *Psychologies*   v

INTRODUCTION   1

1: WHAT DOES REAL CALM MEAN TO YOU?   7

CHAPTER 1:   Defining real calm   9
TAKE THE TEST: *What does real calm mean to you?*   25

CHAPTER 2:   Why do you want to be calm?   31
TAKE THE TEST: *How does lack of calm affect your life?*   48

CHAPTER 3:   How does real calm *really* feel?   55

2: WHAT'S STOPPING YOU FROM
   FEELING CALM?   69

CHAPTER 4:   What's at the root of your stress?   71
TAKE THE TEST: *What is really stressing you out?*   86

CHAPTER 5:   Understanding your mind: when to
                  seek help   93
TAKE THE TEST: *How do you handle stress?*   108

CHAPTER 6:   Stress triggers   113

3: HOW CAN YOU BE CALM?   129

CHAPTER 7:   Can you learn to be calm?   131
CHAPTER 8:   Living your own version of calm   145
CHAPTER 9:   Calm boosters   157
CHAPTER 10:   Keep calm and carry on every day   177

WHAT NEXT?   191
ABOUT *PSYCHOLOGIES*   193
REFERENCES   195

FOREWORD

by Suzy Greaves, Editor, *Psychologies*

Many of us are struggling with self-doubt, worry and overwhelm on a daily basis and the aim of this book is to give you a set of tools, tests, techniques and questions to help you to discover how to make some real changes to create real calm in your life.

What *is* real calm? At *Psychologies,* we believe that creating calm in your life starts with becoming more self-aware. It's about being able to identify what is causing you stress in your life – be it your own negative self-talk or external circumstances – and then finding new ways to deal with how you feel.

It's about taking responsibility for what you decide to put your attention on, and deciding not to give absolute authority to the thoughts that may constantly chip away at your equilibrium.

Real Calm is about learning to be in the present, to breathe and focus on what is really going on right here, right now – versus being haunted by the past or catastrophizing about the future.

Real Calm is also about identifying when you need extra support if feeling stressed has drifted into a chronic condition that might spiral downwards if you don't seek help.

You can't always control what happens to you, but *Real Calm* is about empowering yourself to decide how you react to stress. It's about being able to recognize stressful situations and learning how to influence your attitude. It will take time and attention but you can train yourself to do this. And that has to be the ultimate freedom.

Enjoy!

Suzy Greaves, Editor, *Psychologies*

Welcome to *Real Calm* – and let's start by breathing.

If there's one thing you want in your frantic life right now, it's to feel calm. And since you're reading this, it's probably fair to say you're taking the matter seriously. We're excited you've taken this step forward because we have the tools that *can* and *will* help you.

Our lives today are apparently busier than ever. What do most people moan about? 'I'm so busy.' And what does that go hand in hand with? 'I'm so stressed.' There may be significant reasons for you to be carrying more responsibility than you are able to deal with. In a climate of corporations making severe cutbacks, how can you be calm when your job pushes you to your physical and mental limits, which then affects your personal life? The paradox is that even when life is good, feeling calm can still be elusive. Whatever your circumstances, you wonder why you don't feel calm.

First, you're not alone. If there's one thing that unites everybody in modern life to one degree or another it's the umbrella of stress. Keeping on top of everything in a life driven by technology, chronic worry about finances in an uncertain economy, anxiety fuelled by uncertainty in life, and the stress of daily life from commuting to dealing with difficult people and situations are universal issues we are all familiar with.

Anxiety, an extreme form of stress, is a mass epidemic, a condition that has somehow crept up on our society. A recent government report[1] revealed that teenage stress is at an all-time high, and significantly higher than the last investigation in 2005.

According to Anxiety UK,[2] one in ten adults in the UK has suffered from debilitating anxiety at some point in their lives. In the past 14 years diagnoses for an anxiety-related condition have increased by nearly 13%. Government figures[3] show that in 2014/15, stress was the reason for a staggering 35% of all work-related sickness, and 43% of all working days lost due to ill health. In America,[4] 18% of the population suffers officially from anxiety. A 2015 poll[5] found that one in four Americans were experiencing stress in their lives and had been through one stressful event in the previous year. And that's the official figures.

There's a need right now for global calm and a need for individual calm. The recession may be over officially, but buying a home and managing financially are huge concerns. Then there's the fact that terrorism is a real threat and we are on a mass alert. Travelling for business or pleasure now comes with added precautions imposed on us, like longer security checks at airports.

Is it possible to be calm in a world that is anything but calm? This is a real issue. There is nothing we can do about natural disasters, from tsunamis to earthquakes, but as individuals we can learn to ease the process of living and feeling as human beings.

We hope that this book will guide you out of stress into feeling calm whenever you need this.

HOW TO USE THIS BOOK

We've divided this book into three parts:

1. What Does Real Calm Mean To You?
2. What's Stopping You From Feeling Calm?
3. How Can You Be Calm?

In Part One you'll get to grips with the real reasons you don't feel calm and how this affects you on a daily and long-term basis. You may be surprised to learn that there are differences in why you *want* to be calm and why you *need* to be calm. You'll become clear about what exactly you're looking for so that the concept of calm is far from abstract.

In Part Two we'll dive into the complex reasons that have brought you to the point of feeling this stressed. You'll be able to unravel the different states of mind so that you can begin to find your unique calm way.

In Part Three we show you exactly what you need to learn and master so that first you can protect yourself from getting into a frazzled state, and second you can develop a sense of calm every day when you need it.

Throughout the book there are simple suggestions for small changes that will lead to noticeable differences in your daily life and help you accumulate a sense of calm. With every step of our analysis there is guidance on how to switch from allowing the process of stress to take over, to embracing calming processes.

At the end of the Chapters 1, 2, 4 and 5, there are tests that will help you assess yourself. There are also 'Ask Yourself' questions to help you reflect and analyse how you feel, so that you can relate each chapter to your personal experience. In this way you can be your own coach.

You will also find case studies from real people who have found different ways to manage stress, harness it in a productive way, and additionally feel better in themselves. (All names and identifying circumstances have been changed.)

We are very excited about the selected panel of six leading experts we have interviewed for this book. Each expert has a particular expertise, knowledge, experience and perspective so that you can gain a thorough understanding of stress, and have a choice of what advice resonates most with you.

The advice in this book goes deep into the body, the brain, the mind – and the way forward requires commitment to change on your part. We do hope that the evidence we have will motivate you to make the commitment – and that you will be excited to do so.

THE EXPERTS INTERVIEWED FOR
REAL CALM

Miriam Akhtar, positive psychologist

Miriam Akhtar is one of the UK's leading positive psychology practitioners. She has created a number of pioneering programmes based on the science of wellbeing, ranging from Positive Youth to Positive Ageing. She is one of 100 experts who contributed to the *World Book of Happiness*.

She is the author of four books including *Positive Psychology for Overcoming Depression* (Watkins). Her new book *What is Post-Traumatic Growth?* (Watkins) is published in 2017.

www.positivepsychologytraining.co.uk
@pospsychologist

Ed Halliwell, mindfulness teacher and writer

Ed Halliwell is one of this country's most popular mindfulness teachers. As well as leading courses in London, Sussex and Surrey, he has introduced mindfulness to major organizations and is an advisor to an All-Party Parliamentary Group to develop mindfulness-based policies for the UK.

He has written the Be Mindful report for the Mental Health Foundation, co-authored one book and written two other books including his latest, *Into The Heart of Mindfulness* (Piatkus).

www.edhalliwell.com
@EdHalliwell

Professor Ian Robertson, psychologist and neuroscientist

Professor Robertson is one of world's leading researchers on neuropsychology. He is a clinical psychologist, neuroscientist and professor at Trinity College Dublin, and founding director of Trinity College Institute of Neuroscience and Co-Director of the Global Brain Health Institute.

He has written over 500 papers on the brain and behaviour and four internationally successful books. His latest book is *The Stress Test – How Pressure Can Make You Stronger and Stronger* (Bloomsbury)

www.ianrobertson.org
www.professorianrobertson.wordpress.com
@ihrobertson

Jeremy Stockwell, performance consultant and TV coach

Jeremy Stockwell is one the UK's leading performance consultants. His clients include high-profile presenters, actors, business leaders, pop stars and politicians. He is a long serving member of the teaching faculty at The Royal Academy of Dramatic Art.

His on-screen credits include the BAFTA award-winning series *Faking It, Strictly Come Dancing* and *How Do You Solve A Problem Like Maria?* His BBC2 series *The Speaker* was critically acclaimed.

www.jeremystockwell.co.uk
www.jeremystockwellcoaching.com
@jeremystockwell

Sandra Elsdon Vigon, Jungian psychotherapist

Sandra Elsdon Vigon has been a psychotherapist in private practice for 30 years, working in Los Angeles and London. She is a member of the British Association of Counselling and Psychotherapy and the California Association of Marriage and Family Therapists.

She has six years post-graduate training at the Analyst Training Program of the C.G. Jung Institute of Los Angeles. Her special interests are dreamwork, the creative process and collage.

www.sandravigon.co.uk

Charlie Walker-Wise, RADA in Business trainer

Charlie Walker-Wise trained as an actor at the Royal Academy of Dramatic Art, and worked in TV, film and theatre. He moved from acting into directing theatre and simultaneously developing a parallel career as a trainer. He is a client director at RADA in Business.

RADA in Business offers specialist communications training. The company attracts clients from across the public and private sector, including finance, fashion, healthcare and central government.

www.radainbusiness.com
@MrWalkerWise
@RADA_London

1 WHAT DOES REAL CALM MEAN TO YOU?

CHAPTER 1

DEFINING REAL CALM

T he concept of calm can seem abstract and elusive. It's a state of mind that tends to conjure up an image of a sunset from a mountain top or a beach sunrise. And yet you crave that feeling on a more constant level. You know that lighting candles and taking long pampering baths offers tranquility, but you're after something deeper.

In the first instance, feeling calm probably means not feeling the way you do right now: worried, anxious, stressed or possibly depressed. All of these states are on a continuum, so although the extremes might be very different, individually they are difficult to distinguish. One thing is for sure, wherever you are on that continuum it doesn't feel good.

If you could somehow not feel *constantly* stressed that would make a huge difference. It's the *constantly* that wears you out – the looping thoughts, the knot in your stomach, the eating too much or not being able to eat, the feeling that you're stuck in a pressure cooker or a boiling kettle. The worst part is having to appear together around other people – like colleagues, bosses or people you manage – and others you have to deal with in daily life, from neighbours to your child's teachers.

In theory you can be honest with friends and family about how you feel, but what if you're too busy to see them? What if you don't want to or can't admit how you feel? What if you don't want to moan or 'bother' them? Or what if you *are* letting off steam or moaning and then feeling guilty?

Modern life is stressful – that's the message we keep receiving, and that's the message we perpetuate. Stress becomes the norm, and if it's the norm and it makes you unhappy then you feel there's something wrong with you. You might be thinking, 'What's wrong with me? Why can't I be calm?' We'll aim to answer these questions in the course of this book.

But let's start with stress. Is modern life really more stressful? Aren't we living longer, finding cures for diseases, looking more youthful and engaging in hobbies and even new careers way into the Third Age (the stage after middle age and before old age)? The answer is complex. Yes, life is better and more advanced in many ways. As stress expert, psychologist and neuroscientist Professor Ian Robertson confirms, life has become less stressful compared to 100 years ago: 'Gone are the days of hunger, daunting high levels of infant and maternal death and diseases like tuberculosis and diphtheria.'

These advances have brought about radical changes. In fact, asking the question whether life is more stressful now than centuries or decades ago is misplaced. How the nature of stress has changed, and how we as individuals and communities deal with stress, are the more pertinent issues.

> " **In some ways modern life is more stressful than it was a hundred years ago. We are faced with fragmented communities, broken families, work pressures and ruthless competition.** "
>
> Professor Ian Robertson, psychologist and neuroscientist

In this chapter we hope to give a starting point for calm that is relevant to life as we live it. You are unique, and what you need to feel calm is not what somebody else needs. By the end of this book we hope that you will be clear on what calm means to you and how to attain this.

CHOOSING WHAT REAL CALM MEANS TO YOU

The word 'calm' originates[1] from the Greek word *kauma* for heat which became *cauma* in Latin for the sun's midday heat, the time to rest and be still. It was adopted in late fourteenth-century French as *calme* for tranquility and quiet, finding its way into late Middle English.

When we hear the word calm in relation to people it's mostly because they need to 'calm down' and stop being angry and agitated, or anxious and stressed. In terms of word associations, calm is bookended with two more words to describe a person who is cool, calm and collected. Who wouldn't want to be described as cool, calm and collected when it's universally considered a positive description?

When we look at synonyms for calm, the words that come up as qualities in people are self-control and self-possession. Yet if we go back to the origin of the word calm, there's no control in the midday heat is there? The same sea that is rough can also be calm – absolutely still with not a single wave. If you associate calm with an innate state of mind this leaves you with no leeway for change. Performance consultant and TV coach Jeremy Stockwell reminds us that 'change is the only constant truth in the universe' and since we too are part of the universe, inevitably everything about us as human beings changes, down to the cells in our bodies.

> **When you are worried, tell yourself: this will change. If you're feeling stressed, tell yourself a little while later you'll feel calm.**
>
> Jeremy Stockwell, performance consultant and TV coach

GET A CALMNESS APP

When leading psychologist and neuroscientist Professor Robertson says he uses an app every day to keep him calm, then you can be sure it works on the mind. The award-winning Buddhify[2] app has meditations to cover everything from waking up to not being able to sleep, from difficult emotions to stressful situations.

Recently, various calmness trackers have been launched so you can monitor exactly how stressed you are and how well you're doing at de-stressing. Spire,[3] developed by Stanford University's Calming Technology Lab, lets you know through vibration when you're tense, focused or calm by measuring your breathing patterns. It's like a fitness tracker that measures your steps. You can monitor which activities or situations affect your stress levels and there are breathing guidelines to help you learn to take action.

Composure comes from the word 'compose', which originally meant to form something through putting together elements, and then came to mean creating music. If you think of calm as (mental) composure, and composure as creating a positive state of mind from the various elements of you, it becomes more attainable.

Equanimity is a wonderful word that means to be calm and composed especially during a difficult situation. It's a word infused with strength, choice and power. One of the worst things about feeling anxious is that it comes with feeling powerless, that sense that everything is happening outside of you and you can't keep up or cope. So if you begin with powerful terminology with equally powerful associations you are empowering yourself.

Once you begin to choose kinder – and in fact more accurate – definitions of calm then it will seem less elusive. So long as it remains a mystery, or something that's always been beyond you, you're setting yourself up for a struggle. And we want to make this as easy for you as possible.

Just as a rough sea will turn calm, so will you.

FINDING SPACE IN A COLLECTIVE TIME OF TURMOIL

One of psychiatrist-psychotherapist Carl Jung's theories was that we all share a collective unconscious. As one of the most influential figures in therapy, this aspect of his philosophy may be particularly pertinent in the time we are living now. The twentieth century experienced two world wars, but once these were over humanity took many strides forward. The very fact that Europe overcame two destructive wars and united is one of them. In the twenty-first century we have mass global concerns from global warming to terrorism, from mass migration as a result of wars, to recession and financial insecurity.

> " **Collectively we are living in a time of turmoil. It's important that as individuals we find a fixed point.** "
>
> Sandra Elsdon Vigon, Jungian psychotherapist

The difference between this time of turmoil compared to previous centuries is that we are too busy as a society to take it all in. When you're perpetually in a state of anxiety and the messages about the world coming at you are anxious also, it's difficult to see either yourself or the world in any positive light. Positive psychologist expert Miriam Akhtar points out that it's necessary to step back, to 'regroup' so that we can see the world as a whole rather than just through 'a red mist'.

Jungian psychotherapist Sandra Elsdon Vigon views individuals in the context of their personal life and of the collective, whether familial or cultural. Collective values today demand that we fill our time with being productive to a point where people feel guilty for taking time out.

" Calm is space – that place or condition or state of no expectation, just being. "

Sandra Elsdon Vigon, Jungian psychotherapist

When there's pressure to be productive at work, and then self-imposed pressure to fill time outside work productively, there is no space for calm. Just by reorienting your interpretation of calm to mean mental space, whether that's staring out of the bus window instead of scrolling through news on your phone, or standing in a garden for a few moments instead of rushing around the house, means you are shifting mental gears. And if we all shifted mental gears and slowed down, how might that be?

How you begin to find that space on a regular basis is a personal choice, and we hope this book will give you some ideas. There is no prescriptive way, but as Vigon stresses you have to find something that helps you. Finding something that gives you mental space is much more attainable than clicking into a state of mind labelled calm.

"Having time to enjoy the moment is what the word calm means for me personally."

Professor Ian Robertson, psychologist and neuroscientist

STRIVING NOT STRUGGLING

Part of life is striving to achieve something better, whether that's a promotion, running a business, buying one's own property, starting a family or exploring a new country every year on vacation. That's what gives us the impetus to get up and go and that's what makes us interesting. It's a process that can feel good because the excitement is mounting. It's satisfying to set yourself the goal of running a marathon to raise money for charity or learning a dance for your wedding. When you get that job, that house, or hit that target for charity, it's a thrill. When stress sets in, though, it casts a veil on what you're striving for. You start to doubt yourself, to worry, and you feel overwhelmed. Instead of striving you're struggling. When life feels like a struggle every day it's like getting up and being pushed down constantly. When this happens you forget what makes you feel good because those feelings are chipped away, and when those feelings are chipped away so is your self-confidence.

Real calm is about being able to feel excited about your life again. It's about reclaiming the you who has lots of options and dreams.

MIRIAM AKHTAR ON FLOURISHING

'Feeling at peace with oneself means feeling good in mind, body and spirit. It's about having a sense of wellbeing, which not only comes from feeling good, but functioning well. This is what it takes to flourish.

For most people, flourishing is also about having peaceful, harmonious interactions. Conflict with others disrupts our sense of harmony.

The moment you start to experience strong negative emotions, your emotional brain takes over and the rational side starts to shut down – and you can't see your world the way you need to. For this you need to have a sense of calm. If you're in the grip of negative emotions like anger and fear, you're less able to work out how best to navigate the world. Negative emotions are a sign of threat and threat puts us on alert which, when it turns into chronic stress, can get in the way of our flourishing.

The more we experience positive emotions like calm, the more we are able to flourish. I like to liken emotions to traffic lights. Emotions act as signals. A negative emotion is a red traffic light which makes us stop and puts us on alert, whereas positive emotions like calm are a signal something is good and we can continue ahead along this road.'

UNDERSTANDING THE TIPPING POINT OF STRESS

The key to figuring out how to be calm is an understanding of what happens to you when you are stressed.

No doubt you've heard of fight or flight – the brain's system of dealing with a threat that will have us putting up a fight when under attack or running for it. The term gets trotted out so much that it's become more of an expression than a scientific term that we need to fully grasp. The brain has an autonomic nervous system which it activates when it registers a threat. A series of neurotransmitters – chemical messengers – are released to alert the body and enable the mind to decide whether to fight the threat or flee from it. When this happens there's high activity in the amygdala, which is the part of the brain that experiences emotions. Anything from a potential car crash to a potential financial problem can activate the entire system.

Professor Robertson explains that 'calmness would be defined as low sympathetic autonomic arousal, low activation of the amygdala and low to moderate levels of [the stress hormone] noradrenaline'. Only it's a lot more complex than that. If we were in this calm state we wouldn't be able to handle life's challenges – good and bad.

Let's say there was a miracle pill and you could permanently be calm. How would you get fired up to go for a promotion at work? How could you motivate your team to win a new client? How could you focus on studying in your spare time for a new qualification? How could you get competitive playing scrabble or a pub quiz or charades?

The fact is we need stress. Too much stress creates health problems and feels wretched, but manageable stress is good for our health and our brain. A recent study[4] published in *Frontiers of Aging Neuroscience* showed that people over 50 who scored highest in having a busy life also had the highest brain function and memory. Studies like this one (by researchers from the Center for Vital Longevity, School of Behavioral and Brain Sciences at the University of Texas and the Department of Psychology at the University of Alabama) are interesting because they provide a full perspective: how the brain is functioning and how the mind is feeling.

PROFESSOR ROBERTSON ON A CALM BRAIN

'When you start to analyse the concept of a calm brain in neuroscientific terms you realize it's a complex process. A journalist in the midst of a coup or war has a different calmness to a tourist lying on a beach.

Take someone who is able to keep a cool head in a crisis. That person could be described as calm, but the sympathetic nervous system will still be activated – the heart will be pumping away. That person might be operating at the sweet spot of arousal, where their cognitive appraisal of the emergency situation is such that they can, in spite of the activation of arousal systems of the body and brain, function at the optimal level where the brain performs at its best.

Feeling able to be in the moment is a better definition of calm than one based on the autonomic arousal, because you can still be performing with high levels of demands without going beyond the sweet spot of arousal, so you can have mindful appraisal of moment to moment events.'

What we don't need is excessive stress. Just like there's good and bad cholesterol and the good cholesterol is essential for the body to function, there's good and bad stress. Excessive stress is bad because you're struggling to cope. Once you are aware that stress is a chemical reaction in your brain, you become more conscious of the ingredients that create the stress. Then you can be conscious that it's the level of stress that pushes you over the limit, or the particular type of stress. You can monitor your maximum point. It's a little like understanding how an oven works. And you're the dish or the cake. A chemical reaction happens when we follow a recipe, create something and put it in the oven for a certain amount of time. Too little it's raw, too much it's burnt. More of this ingredient it's more moist, less of that ingredient it's lighter.

" Calm is a sufficiently diffuse concept that you can craft it. "

Professor Ian Robertson, psychologist and neuroscientist

As soon as you reformulate your view of stress you can observe yourself and learn not only what triggers you beyond your limit (a burnt you), but what type of situation is best for you (you turn out great). We all need a degree of 'heat' to thrive. You might be feeling that you can't cope well in a competitive work arena, but maybe you love the challenge of learning a language. You might be sick with nerves and have sleepless nights before having to make a presentation, but maybe you're the first one up at karaoke on a night out. You might worry every day about the uncertainty of your future and whether to change jobs or take early redundancy, yet be the fearless joker of your group of friends.

IDENTIFYING WHEN STRESS IS *NOT* THE ISSUE

When we look at people handling stress calmly, the fight or flight system is still activated and enables them to take action. Professor Robertson gathered ample evidence for his latest book *The Stress Test* to back up his conviction that pressure can be good for us – provided we know our sweet spot. One of the many studies he drew our attention to was a Chicago University experiment[5] that demonstrated the importance of confidence while stressed. A group of students equally good at maths had to solve problems in front of an audience. Half were confident, the other half weren't. Both groups produced the stress hormone cortisol, but the confident group did better. As Professor Robertson writes 'the more of the stress hormone they produced, the BETTER they performed'.

Gee, thanks, you might be thinking if you're not confident. But the point we want to highlight here is that for the group that didn't do so well, it was not stress that created the problem but a lack of something else. And that something else might be easier to cultivate than an intangible calmness. The question to consider is whether it's calm you lack when you're wrecked with nerves, or something else like confidence. And if it's confidence (as our *Real Confidence* book outlines), you can most easily develop this through focusing on learning the skill you don't yet have, whether it's public speaking or managing a team, or taking maths tests in a laboratory for scientists. Competence can make you calm.

IDENTIFY YOUR REAL STRENGTHS AND TURN THESE INTO POSITIVE AFFIRMATIONS

One of the most common areas of potential stress comes from dealing with people in a more powerful position, like bosses or clients. In these instances, being clear about your strengths and affirming them to yourself can help you navigate yourself through the situation. Before an update with your manager, a pitch to a client, an appraisal meeting with human resources, for example, take time to identify your strengths and repeat them to yourself.

The idea of a tipping point in our brain is in fact a cornerstone of psychology. Harvard psychologists Robert Yerkes and John Dodson[6] came up with the concept of an arousal curve in the brain in 1908. They discovered that arousal – which Professor Robertson explains is alertness in the brain – can improve performance, but if the increase goes beyond a tipping point then performance is affected negatively. Scientists have since studied the Yerkes–Dodson theory in different contexts.

Knowing your tipping point, or rather your tipping points for different situations in life, means you can use your brain's alertness to create excitement in your life without going to the point that leaves you feeling unwell, exhausted and unable to manage your life.

That 'thing' that makes humans excited and competitive is in our minds. Too little and you wouldn't be doing much with your life, too much and life is overwhelming.

Once you realize that you don't need or want to be calm all the time, then feeling calm becomes more attainable.

ED HALLIWELL ON THE STATE OF CALM VS THE SKILL OF CALM

'There's calm as a state which we maybe think of as a feeling of peace and tranquility, a sense of not being on high alert and an absence of anxiety. It's a feeling of settledness.

Then there's calm as a trait – the capacity to manage the inevitable difficulties of being alive. It's important to recognize life as being difficult (as well as having many joys potentially). Then calm doesn't mean the absence of difficulties but instead is a willingness and capacity to be with the difficulties and work with them, rather than trying to fight them and get away from them.

Being calm doesn't require a state of calm to be there in your life or even in your mind and body. You can learn how to manage life in a calm way. A deeper calm can come from working with difficulties in life.

The difficulty is that if we are defining calm as a feeling, then when we are not completely in control of what comes up in our life, we can't magic a feeling of peace. And sometimes during difficult times calm isn't helpful because actions have to be taken. You don't want to be calm when a bus is coming at you – you need to be hyper alert so that your body gets you out of the way.

Calm as a state may be overrated. But a different kind of calm that is a way of relating with life's difficulties is a valuable skill to cultivate.'

We hope that our approach to defining real calm is one that immediately makes you feel you're not so far from it. If you view calm people as those people you can't be like because of the hullabaloo in your head, then you're tormenting yourself with an unattainable vision. The starting point is choosing empowering interpretations of the word. Just because stress can feel like it's constant doesn't mean that the antidote is constant calmness. Real calm is a skill you call on when you need it. And in a world that's anything but calm we need to carve out space to restore ourselves, to maintain our inner equilibrium.

Real calm comes down to feeling good about life. When you're flourishing in your life, you can handle pressure and are able to thrive on the right amount of stress. Understanding the chemistry of stress, and specifically learning how much you can handle to thrive and where your tipping point lies, can propel you forward to achieve your ambitions and enjoy life. Ultimately real calm is a skill rather than a state of mind. It's a skill we hope you are keen to master through reading the rest of this book.

ASK YOURSELF

Q   What does the word calm conjure up for you?

Q   What is the opposite of calm for you?

Q   What happens in your body when you are not calm? What are the sensations?

Q   In which areas of your life would like to be calm?

Q   When are you calm?

WHAT DOES REAL CALM MEAN TO YOU?

You picked up this book for a reason. You know it's time to make changes, but the key to successfully achieving any change is to 'start with the end in mind'. So before you read on, it's worth taking the time to think about what 'being calm' really means to you. What do you hope to gain from changing your mindset? What are the most important changes you hope it will bring? As you work through this book, you will begin to build a picture of how you would like your optimal life to look and feel, and how different it will be from the way you live now. Start by taking this test to identify the most important benefits for you of reconnecting with your sense of calm.

Test by Sally Brown

QUESTION 1

When the alarm goes on Monday morning, you're most likely to think:

A. Why do weekends go so fast?
B. What is there to look forward to this week?
C. If only I could get up and meditate …
D. Healthy living starts today!

QUESTION 2

On your last holiday, you most appreciated:

A. The time to unwind and not rush.
B. Eating well, being active and getting decent sleep.
C. Putting worries and responsibilities on hold and enjoying life.
D. The chance to think about the bigger picture.

QUESTION 3

Finish this sentence. The key to calm is:

A. Feeling connected, like you belong.
B. Living a balanced lifestyle.
C. Self-acceptance and self-worth.
D. Good physical and mental health.

QUESTION 4

What do you crave most when you're feeling under pressure?

A. Time on your own.
B. Laughter and lightheartedness.
C. Everything that's bad for you.
D. Support from someone insightful.

QUESTION 5

What's changed the most since you've lost your sense of calm?

A. Your overall mood and mindset.

B. Your health and physical wellbeing.

C. Your focus and memory.

D. Your relationships and social life.

QUESTION 6

Which of these changes would make you feel more on top of things?

A. Regular coaching or counselling sessions.

B. Being more efficient about getting things done.

C. Spending more time with like-minded people.

D. Having more motivation and energy.

QUESTION 7

Which of these statements would you agree with the most?

A. Physical health is the foundation of mental wellbeing.

B. A sense of purpose is the foundation of happiness.

C. A busy life is not the same as a successful one.

D. Life is short, so it's important to enjoy it.

QUESTION 8

Which advice do you get most often?

A. 'You need to let your hair down.'

B. 'You need to learn how to say no.'

C. 'You need to take better care of yourself.'

D. 'You need to lower your standards.'

QUESTION 9

What aspect of your life suffers the most when you're not calm?

A. Your health and eating habits.
B. Your sense of direction and purpose.
C. Your general mood and sense of humour.
D. Your sense of peace and feeling in control.

QUESTION 10

Which of these brings the most noticeable change to your mood?

A. Having a really good laugh.
B. A meeting or other commitment being cancelled.
C. A yoga class or going for a walk.
D. Feeling like you've achieved something.

Now, add up your scores from each answer using the following table, and read on to discover what real calm means to you.

	A	B	C	D
Q1	6	8	2	4
Q2	4	2	6	8
Q3	2	6	8	6
Q4	2	6	4	8
Q5	8	4	2	6
Q6	6	8	4	2
Q7	2	4	6	8
Q8	8	6	4	2
Q9	4	2	8	6
Q10	2	4	6	8

If you scored between 20 and 35 …

Real calm for you means reconnecting with fun

Losing touch with your sense of humour is a red flag for you – a sign that you are under pressure or feeling out of control. You may be outwardly functioning, but life feels flat, and it can feel like you're just going through the motions a lot of the time. It's only when you experience moments of calm that you find yourself laughing easily again. For you, feeling calm is about reconnecting with your sense of humour and upbeat approach to life.

Something may have changed in recent months – in your working life, family or friendships – which has affected your natural exuberance and enthusiasm for life. There are times when you have to work through a low period, but for you, the catch-22 is that when you lose touch with your sense of fun, you also lose your emotional resilience. It's time to reconnect with calm, and give yourself permission to feel happy again.

If you scored between 36 and 45 …

Real calm for you means time slowing down

When you're under pressure, time seems to speed up. It can feel like your life becomes a treadmill and you're using all your energies just to keep up. Days pass by in a blur and, even though you always seem to be busy, you never get through your to-do list. You are craving the chance to think big picture – at the moment, you have no idea what direction your life is taking. Perhaps you picked up this book because you realized that another year had passed without you getting closer to your goals, or even clarifying what those goals really are and committing to them. Instinctively, you have identified that reconnecting with your inner calm is the key to slowing down time and feeling more in control of your life. If you start each day by asking yourself what you need to do that day, try a different question – ask yourself, how do you *want* to feel today?

If you scored between 46 and 60 ...
Real calm for you means better choices

For you, being calm is the foundation of good life choices, whether it's what to eat, how much to drink, and how to make time for exercise and other lifestyle choices like mindfulness. When you lose your sense of calm, you also lose control and go into self-sabotage mode, and your lifestyle can quickly become chaotic. When you feel calmer, you tend to compensate by going into super-health mode. But you've recognized that yo-yoing between extremes isn't a sustainable way to live. You're looking for balance. Your first step is to stop resisting the uncomfortable feelings that come up for you when you feel stressed. Try making space for them, ask: 'What are these feelings trying to tell me?' and start to listen.

If you scored between 61 and 80 ...
Real calm for you means flourishing

You've done a lot of soul-searching of late and come to the conclusion that the key to becoming your best self is feeling calmer and more in control in everyday life. You have instinctively identified that reducing your stress levels will help you think more positively, and feel motivated about reaching your potential. You feel like you're on the cusp of flourishing and becoming your best self, so it's frustrating that it remains just out of reach. Taking a step back from striving and, instead, reconnecting with your inner calm will help you focus and see your clear path forward.

CHAPTER 2

WHY DO YOU WANT TO BE CALM?

ow this might seem like a silly question. You want to be calm because right now doesn't feel good. Getting to the core of why you want to be calm is a significant first step into that nebulous cloud that lies between your current state and the one you desire. Once we have helped you delve deeper, you will find the process easier.

We're well aware that when you feel stressed, calm is a wished for state. In this chapter we will explore what's behind your desire to overcome stress. Real calm is knowing what exactly this means to you as an individual because, like the word healthy, it means different things to different people.

YOU WANT TO FEEL LIKE THAT HOLIDAY-YOU

You might be the sort of person who instantly unwinds when you're on holiday. Or like most people it could take you some time before you fully relax. Perhaps you're someone who can't let go of periodically checking the work email or gets agitated when the hotel Wi-Fi isn't working. Whichever type you are, one thing is for sure: there will be moments on holiday when you experience something other than what you go through on a daily basis during your normal routine. You might not label this as calm. Instead you're likely to find yourself saying: *I feel like me again*. These are the moments or the periods when you like yourself. Go on then, you *really* like yourself. You return home and want to keep the holiday feeling going. Only how to stay calm when the email inbox is bursting, your boss is making demands, your team are playing up, the trains are delayed or aren't running, your children or parents are sick, your teenagers have disappointed you, and one of your utilities has overcharged you? Is it any wonder you finally lose it over the neighbour's rubbish?

And so the cycle begins. Stress takes over your life. One way or another, you get used to it and tell yourself that you can't change work-life, society or the economy. This is how it is. The problem is that once this line of thinking sets in another set of beliefs develops: *Well it must be me; if this is life and I'm stressed, agitated, low, unhappy, then there must be something wrong with me.* And then you go on holiday, remember who you are, remember that no, there's nothing wrong with you, and you try once again. With each new cycle negative beliefs become more entrenched: *I'm alright on holiday but that's not real life; real life is frantic and busy; I can't cope with real life, I'm permanently stressed; what's wrong?*

> **On the whole you can't run away from life. And if you can't do anything about the difficulties you're facing, this can ramp up the stress.**
>
> Ed Halliwell, mindfulness teacher and writer

If you think in terms of keeping Holiday-You present throughout your busy life, that's more tangible. Instead of wanting to be calm, you could ask yourself what you need to be even a little more You. Only *you* know what that is – is it wearing colourful clothes, or telling jokes, not nagging your partner or giving a damn about work outside work? Could you slow down just a little bit? Can you reduce your busyness by even 1%?

> **Everyone can find 30 seconds to stop and breathe instead of checking Facebook. You will feel more in control, and control is the antidote to anxiety.**
>
> Professor Ian Robertson, psychologist and neuroscientist

33

You want: To always be that Holiday-You
You need: To find ways to always be You

YOU'RE TIRED OF BEING TOO BUSY

You might be in a situation where life isn't bad, where everything is going super-well, and if anything there's too much of a good thing, or rather too many exciting things going on. You never stop moving, thinking, doing. And instead of enjoying what's good you may have a low-level anxiety. You're not alone.

Rushing has become part of our modern city culture, and being busy is virtually a badge of achievement. When was the last time you told anyone you were bored? When was the last time you announced you had nothing to do? Come to think of it, how many people tell you or post on their Facebook timeline that they're doing absolutely nothing? Even if you are doing nothing there's a sense of having to chronicle it with a perfect Instagram or Facebook post.

"We need to consciously make space in our busy-ness to create calm."

Sandra Elsdon Vigon, Jungian psychotherapist

In Chapter 1, psychologist and neuroscientist Professor Robertson explained that there's a sweet spot for stress and if we're aware of this, we can be outwardly calm but inwardly fired up to take positive actions. An awareness of where your sweet spot is can be down to the optimum level of busy-ness for you. If your job is pressurized and outside work you've set yourself the challenge of overcoming two left feet and learning to dance – and you're also breaking up from a relationship and moving – you are most certainly overdoing things.

It's worth bearing in mind that studies on willpower (one of the most researched areas in psychology) show that our willpower reserves are finite. Willpower guru Roy Baumeister[1] advises resting, sleeping and eating well to fuel willpower because our reserves are drained by the demands of everyday life plus unexpected demands.[2] To cultivate your calm self will require willpower. You might have to start changing your habits, taking on fewer commitments, saying no and reducing your busy-ness to a level that suits you.

> *You want: To handle being 'so busy' calmly*
> *You need: To reduce the busy-ness*

YOU JUST WANT TO BE HAPPY

When stress becomes so invasive that you lie awake anxiously and feel miserable all the time it's inevitable that you associate finding calmness with happiness.

A more useful appraisal of happiness is to think of Hungarian psychologist Mihály Csíkszentmihályi's mental state of flow.[3] Csíkszentmihályi's studies found that when we're in a state of flow, regardless of what we're doing, we don't want to be doing anything else – we lose all sense of time and are fully absorbed. Mindfulness expert Ed Halliwell agrees with Csíkszentmihályi's concept that 'similarly, happiness is a state of not wanting to be in another state'.

This comes back to cultivating the skill of calm in order to handle whatever it is that's making you unhappy, tackling how to make changes, coming up with a plan, gaining support and seeing it through. Being fixated on going from stressed to calm in order to be happy is like being stuck in a car that won't start, desperate to arrive at a magical destination – without knowing what's wrong with the car and which destination would make you feel happy. First you need to fix the car and then consider your route and destination. Yes, that might be a slow drive through sleepy, scenic surroundings arriving at a blissful place. But equally it could be an adrenaline fuelled race along the motorway to a bustling, vibrant city.

You want: To be happy

You need: To know what you need to be happy

MIRIAM AKHTAR ON UNDERSTANDING POSITIVE EMOTIONS SO WE CAN CULTIVATE THEM

'There's an epidemic of stress in the twenty-first century.

We're not just expected to juggle all the time, with the addition of smartphones and social media we are multi-juggling. People are very easily overwhelmed because of the multiple demands on our attention and that's a source of more negative emotion.

We live in a time of impermanence. Permanence gave us greater security in employment and relationships, whereas now there is much less sense of certainty and security which leads to stress. Insecurity at so many levels in these uncertain times drives a lot of stress. It's not surprising that we feel so many negative emotions.

The problem with all these negative emotions is that, compared to positive ones, they are bigger experiences – they feel louder and in your face, so they wear you down and hold you in fear. Positive emotions are lighter and fleeting. It's because they are fleeting that we need to work harder to experience them. We need to cultivate these positive emotions because they have a good effect on us.'

YOU WANT YOUR TEAM TO BE CALM

Being promoted to manage a team or getting offered the job of being a manager or leader in a work arena is exciting. But at some point you realize that management is also about managing emotions – other people's. And if they're not calm and you're not calm, covering up your stress to somehow help your team deal with their stress isn't easy, to say the least.

When RADA in Business trainer Charlie Walker-Wise started working with CEOs and business leaders he quickly realized that being a theatre director was an enormous advantage. Leaders, he discovered, are the same whether working in arts and entertainment or the corporate world: 'They are setting a vision, communicating it with passion, bringing together a team, releasing creativity both latent and explicit, giving confidence, and giving people permission to fail.'

> **Actors tell a story in a compelling way and change the way the audience feel. It's the same in business. You tell a story in a compelling way so that people do something differently.**
>
> Charlie Walker-Wise, RADA in Business trainer

All leaders, regardless of whether they were always driven to lead or found themselves managing by accident, have enormous responsibilities, demands, packed diaries. There is never enough time. And that's just work. If your team are frantically trying to cope and are making yet more demands on you or letting you down, you have the double challenge of handling their stress and yours.

You want: Your team to calm down

You need: To let your team experience you as calm

YOU WISH YOU COULD SHUT DOWN YOUR MIND

When stress becomes chronic it can feel like you have a permanent scream in your head that you want to escape from. If only you could shut down your mind. The most common way people deal with this feeling is to have a drink or two, or more. Alcohol, however, doesn't address or solve the stress. It takes the edge off and in excess creates other problems.

It's vital to get to the heart of the stress matter because long-term stress damages the body's ability to manage health, including the heart. How the brain affects health is a relative new area of scientific research. Even though scientists are still exploring this, in the past few years a number of studies have underlined that there most definitely is a link between the two.

A groundbreaking 2012 study[4] by Professor of Psychology Sheldon Cohen at Carnegie Mellon University discovered that the effect of chronic psychological stress is that the body loses its ability to manage inflammation, so the result is the onset of disease. This is because we need the hormone cortisol to deal with the inflammation – but if it's called on by the brain to deal with mental stress, then it can't do all its work. An earlier study by Cohen focused on the common cold, demonstrating that it's the body's inflammatory response to the virus that leads to an actual cold, rather than the virus itself – which is why you're more likely to catch a cold when you're run down.

A recent major and in-depth study by the Center for Healthy Aging and Department of Biobehavioral Health,[5] Penn State, found that adults who don't keep calm have higher levels of inflammation in the body. Moreover, women are at a greater risk. Inflammation leads to obesity as well as serious health disorders like heart problems and cancer.

What's groundbreaking about the above study is the finding that it's not the level or frequency of stress that is damaging to the body, but the mental response to it that creates the inflammation. While most research looks at chronic stress or laboratory-induced stress, this study focused on everyday situations including arguments and avoiding arguments at work. If you are feeling that conflict wears you down, then you can be assured through this research that your sense is entirely justified. It really is wearing out your body and it's essential to find ways to deal with the problem.

ED HALLIWELL ON THE DISCREPANCY MONITOR IN YOUR MIND

'Professor of psychology and former director of the Oxford Mindfulness Centre, Mark Williams, developed the concept of a discrepancy monitor in mindfulness based cognitive therapy. When we perceive that something has gone wrong, our thinking minds have a way of trying to sort it out. One of the difficulties with life is that not all things that get us stressed can be fixed with a simple action. Then we start ruminating, we feel more stressed, and the discrepancy becomes the stressor.

Somehow there's the idea now that we're supposed to have it all and be able to live a life that is calm, and that's a discrepancy. Who said we should be calm? If you don't have that sense that you should be calm, then you don't have a discrepancy looping through your mind.'

Identifying what triggers you is not only helpful, it's also essential for your body's health. Here are some pretty alarming figures, but the awareness will give you the incentive to avoid being triggered to the extent of an angry outburst. A 2015 study at the University of Sydney[6] investigated emotional triggers and heart attacks and found that the risk of a heart attack is 8.5 times higher during the two hours after an angry outburst. The study also showed that episodes of anxiety increase the risk of triggering a heart attack by 9.5 times. Patients admitted to hospital were interviewed about their activities in the 48 hours before admission. Though it may be reassuring that only 2% of the sample experienced an 'anger-triggered' heart attack, those who did were at a significantly higher risk. The study's conclusions were that people with heart disease need stress reduction training in addition to health advice on diet and giving up smoking.

Finding inner calm can literally reduce health risks, while worrying can make you more ill. Research published in the *Journal of the American College of Cardiology*[7] (*JACC*) in 2007 outlined the benefits of relieving anxiety for people suffering from heart disease. Relieving anxiety helps to further erode disease. The three-year study involved patients suffering from coronary artery disease recording their feelings. Those who scored high in anxiety had almost double the risk of heart attack or death.

Our objective is to steer you to take measures so that you manage the stress that can potentially lead to heart disease in the first place. If there's a family history, it's an issue that may already be on your radar. When someone or something upsets you, now that you know the latest research on the links between mind and body you can ask yourself whether your long-term health is worth this something or someone. This question in itself will lead you to take actions.

We believe that finding ways to be calm is as important as watching your cholesterol. If you're full of angst about your weight, finding ways to feel calm will do far more for your figure than trying out another diet. Investing long term in your health, even if you feel you're too young to be worrying about heart problems and cancer, is as smart as measures like saving for an emergency or your own property, paying into a pension or a savings scheme.

You want: Relief for your mind

You need: To take control of your mind so that your body can be healthy

TRICK YOUR BODY

Though you can't *tell* yourself you are calm because the brain doesn't believe it, there is scientific evidence that you can *trick* your brain through your body. Professor Robertson draws attention to the science that proves that simple physical activities boost the brain so we feel calm. Simply squeezing a rubber ball[8] in your right hand boosts the left 'approach' side of your brain so you take more action and are less prone to low moods. (Squeeze for 45 seconds, release for 15 and repeat.) And social psychologist Amy Cuddy's research[9] has demonstrated that just two minutes a day of putting yourself in an open posture triggers positive changes in brain chemistry including raising testosterone and boosting dopamine levels. (Make sure your head is straight ahead of you, your shoulders are even, and spread your arms away from your armpits to occupy space.)

YOU WANT TO BE YOUR BEST AT WORK

Jungian psychotherapist Sandra Elsdon Vigon says that after three decades of working in Los Angeles and London she has noticed that technology has changed people dramatically. 'At the beginning of a session, it often takes clients 15–20 minutes to land in their body. I liken this to a flock of birds circling overhead, looking for a place to land.'

Of course it's easy to blame addiction to social media and a reliance on email and texting for the effect technology has on us. But there's also the change in the work culture. For when does the work day end? A recent study led by associate professor of management Liuba Belkin at Lehigh University[10] is the first to demonstrate a link between emotional exhaustion and after-hour work email demands. The study 'Exhausted, but unable to disconnect: the impact of email-related organizational expectations on work-family balance' highlights the need for corporations to change their demands. Dealing with work emails at all times creates what the study terms anticipatory stress, which is a constant state of anxiety.

Working excessive hours damages rather than boosts your work performance. It may appear efficient to be responding to emails after official hours, but this keeps your body in the stress mode and prevents you relaxing. Consider ways to limit email contact when you leave the office (like setting a cut-off time in the evening, switching on when you're on your commute instead of first thing when you wake up, and sticking to a strict weekend window of time). You might consider showing the above research to your manager or Human Resources.

" Stress occurs when demands made on you exceed your ability to satisfy these. If you are asked to do more than you can the result is anxiety. And anxiety reduces your ability to manage stress. "

Professor Ian Robertson, psychologist and neuroscientist

How we react in stressful work situations doesn't alter our ability, yet it does influence performance. One study by the Rotman School of Management[11] found that calm candidates did better in job application tests. Of course that's common sense, anyone could have guessed that. But it's interesting that the report published in the *Journal of Applied Psychology* recommended actively seeking ways to minimize anxiety. This of course won't be a surprise to you if you find that your abilities are hampered because you get into an anxious state, and then feel frustrated because colleagues less able than you but more confident get promoted. At least you know now this isn't in your head. Mastering ways to reduce anxiety and induce calm, plus your ability, will transform your opportunities at work.

You want: To perform better at work

You need: To eliminate work demands outside work and focus on finding relaxing activities

WHEN YOU ARE CALM YOU CAN COPE

When life gets too much and everything feels as if it's going wrong, at the same time you need a clear head: to make a plan, to get support, to keep your job going and/or to be a responsible parent. But as you have probably already experienced, your mind is fraught and exhausted from running mental marathons on a loop.

"When people are suffering they need help because the pain is intolerable. "

Sandra Elsdon Vigon, Jungian psychotherapist

One of the main reasons people want to be calm, and this might resonate with you, is because life can feel like a daily suffering. Sometimes it's obvious what that suffering is due to, but when it's not so obvious this can feel terribly frightening. When worry becomes chronic and is consistently present in your life you live anticipating the worst.

In his latest book, mindfulness teacher Ed Halliwell charts his own journey of finding relief from suffering, describing with admirable clarity, empathy and humility his struggle of overcoming a hollow melancholy feeling, a 'vague premonition of a fearful future'.[12] Despite being a 'meditation failure' to start with, Halliwell embarks on a journey of healing through the mind and describes feeling 'calm' after crying at a retreat. What's reassuring about Halliwell's journey is his message that to some degree this suffering is a universal condition.

TALK ON THE PHONE WITH SOMEONE SUPPORTIVE

Call someone who is able to give you support when you need this. This could be an understanding partner, but it could also be an older, more experienced mentor. Texting isn't the same, as one study confirms.

Biological anthropologist Leslie Seltzer at the University of Wisconsin-Madison[13] studied a group of 7- to 12-year-old girls in the stressful situation of making an unprepared speech and solving maths problems in front of a panel of strangers. A third of the girls were comforted in person by their mums, a third watched a neutral 75-minute video and the rest were given a phone with their mums on the line. The children who were physically with their mothers had the same hormonal response as the ones who spoke to their mothers, with levels of oxytocin (the bonding hormone) rising, and cortisol (the stress hormone) falling.

As we highlighted in Chapter 1, there's the state of calm and the skill of calm – and cultivating the skill of calm empowers you so that you can deal with whatever life is throwing at you. There are stressful events that can't be avoided, like a loved one suffering from a disease and bereavement. We need to keep our reserves so that we can keep going through unavoidable stressful events. In Chapter 1 we outlined what happens in the brain when we are stressed: it activates the fight or flight response. The one thing our brain can't do, despite its sophistication, is tell the difference between a mortal threat and not being able to find your keys. You may very well be experiencing that being on constant alert wears you down.

> **Any problem, from a full inbox or a noisy neighbour, to illness, activates the threat-detector in our minds.**
>
> Ed Halliwell, mindfulness teacher and writer

The brain needs to be calm because of the way it's affected by stress. An interesting study by two neuroscientists at Louisiana State University's Health Sciences Center New Orleans in 2011[14] showed that the area of the brain involved in memory and learning can be affected negatively through being exposed to just one incident of acute stress.

One of the reasons we are confident you will benefit from this book is because of the scientific evidence that the brain is 'plastic'. The brain can change. However, just as the brain's plasticity can be used positively, what this study underlines is that it can also be affected negatively. What we learn from this study is that it's essential to allow time to recover from the stress of extreme events like accidents and bereavement. You need to be calm to boost your brain's ability to handle stress so that its other functions are not affected.

You want: To cope with everything now
You need: To take time to recover

By analysing what it is you really want beyond calm we hope that you can begin to find ways to introduce calm into your life by addressing tangible issues: you want to feel and be the best You, that person who is in a good mood and great to be around on holiday; you want to live life to the full, but not so that you're worn out chasing your tail; you'd like to be doing things that give you pleasure from whatever isn't great in your life; and for all the pressures of the world you'd like to find a way to inspire those around you. You want to live up to your best abilities at work and you want to deal with whatever life throws at you.

You might not have considered why you *need* to be calm and we've highlighted this because, yes, there is a certain urgency to needing it. You need to address finding calm spaces in your life because stress destroys health, and there is ample evidence for this. If you feel you're not coping well at work, at least there is confirmation now that the current work culture of emails outside work creates anxiety and burnout. Rather than pushing yourself and keeping your brain in a constant alert, you'll hopefully now give yourself time to process and recover from any stress beyond your control – like moving, divorce, bereavement, redundancy. Investigating what you need will help you develop specific ways to look after yourself. Real calm comes from a foundation of self-care.

ASK YOURSELF

Ⓠ Having read this chapter is there a difference between why you want to be calm and need to be calm?

Ⓠ Forget calm. What do you want in your life? What do you need in your life?

Ⓠ When you are most frazzled, what do you need during those moments?

Ⓠ Do you experience moments, long periods or constant stress? If constant, is it low or high?

Ⓠ If you're a manager, how do you cover up your own feelings of stress? How do you deal with your team's stress?

HOW DOES LACK OF CALM AFFECT YOUR LIFE?

The key to committing to significant lifestyle changes is understanding your reasons and motivation for changing. This test is designed to help you identify how lack of calm has impacted on your life. Sometimes we have lived with raised stress levels for so long that it becomes the new normal, and we simply lower our expectations of health, wellbeing or quality of life. And sometimes stress can manifest itself in surprising ways. Take this test to find out how the absence of calm is undermining your personal wellbeing, and what you need to do to protect your health and happiness, now and in the future.

Test by Sally Brown

QUESTION 1

Which of these do you find yourself doing when you're low?

A. Binge eating or drinking.

B. Venting to whoever will listen.

C. Random online shopping.

D. Ruminating over past mistakes.

QUESTION 2

Finish this sentence. When I'm calmer, I'll be:

A. In control.

B. A nicer person.

C. More successful.

D. Healthier.

QUESTION 3

Which of the following investments in yourself would bring the most benefit?

A. Sessions with a personal trainer and nutritionist.

B. A top-to-toe health MOT.

C. A course in Cognitive Behaviour Therapy to boost your confidence issues.

D. Life coaching in how to manage stress more effectively.

QUESTION 4

Which of these do you consider your biggest weakness?

A. Niggly health issues.

B. Worry and anxiety.

C. Lack of willpower.

D. Mood swings.

QUESTION 5

Which of the following changes would make you feel more on top of things?

A. Having more time to take care of yourself.
B. Worrying less about everything.
C. Having more energy and just feeling well.
D. Getting on better with friends and family.

QUESTION 6

What's the usual payback when you take on too much?

A. Withdrawing from social events.
B. Picking up every bug going.
C. Putting on weight.
D. Worrying and doubting your ability to cope.

QUESTION 7

You've been offered a promotion which will bring with it an initial period of stress. Which of the following consequences would you worry about the most?

A. The impact on your physical health.
B. The impact on your mental wellbeing.
C. The impact on your relationships.
D. The impact on your weight and how you look.

QUESTION 8

If a good friend was going through a hard time, you'd make them feel better by:

A. Sharing your own problems.
B. Going round with a bottle of wine.
C. Offering a shoulder to cry on.
D. Suggesting they seek professional help.

QUESTION 9

Which of these qualities do you find yourself envying in other people?

A. Self-compassion.

B. Self-reliance.

C. Self-belief.

D. Self-discipline.

QUESTION 10

If things don't change, your secret fear is that you will:

A. Lose your job.

B. Get really fat.

C. End up alone.

D. Develop a serious illness.

Now, add up your scores from each answer using the following table, and read on to discover which aspect of your life is most affected by your current state of mind.

	A	B	C	D
Q1	2	4	8	6
Q2	8	4	6	2
Q3	8	2	6	4
Q4	2	6	8	4
Q5	8	6	2	4
Q6	4	2	8	6
Q7	2	6	4	8
Q8	4	8	6	2
Q9	2	4	6	8
Q10	6	8	4	2

If you scored between 20 and 35 ...

Stress sabotages your health

When you lose your sense of calm, your health is the first thing to suffer, whether it's a flare-up of skin problems, disrupted digestion, or picking up every bug going. Your warning stress sign is finding yourself fantasizing about taking a day off and spending it in bed. Take this as your cue to slow down, and treat yourself with kindness. Think of your health issues as messages from your body. Rather than simply dealing with the symptoms, think about what your body needs – whether that's more sleep, more time outdoors close to nature, or simply more time for rest and recuperation. Try starting the day with a 'body scan' mindfulness exercise, checking in with how you feel. You can then ask yourself, 'What do I need today? What needs to change?'

If you scored between 36 and 45 ...

Stress sabotages your relationships

When you feel calm, you can be great company, with a friendly, outgoing personality. But you find it hard to hide your feelings, so it's a different story when you're under stress. As a 'people-person', you turn to others to help manage your emotions, understand what's going on and feel better. But if you don't get the support you need, you can feel frustrated, and become snappy and irritable. You may find yourself withdrawing emotionally or getting into arguments. When the cause of your stress goes, your normal, friendly personality returns, but it can take time for your relationships to repair. Reconnecting with calm is not just an investment in yourself, it's an investment in the people you care about. By tuning into your stress warning signs before they get out of control, you can learn to self-manage your emotions and reduce the impact of your moods on those you love.

If you scored between 46 and 60 …

Stress sabotages your self-confidence

When you're under stress, you have a tendency to see the world through a mental filter – it edits out any evidence that you're coping and doing well and spotlights what you see as mistakes and weaknesses instead. You often keep your concerns to yourself but, at the same time, you crave reassurance from other people. When you're at your most stressed, you may have a tendency to go into black and white thinking mode, or catastrophize ('I'm so out of my depth, I'm going to mess up everything and lose my job'). So your first priority is to regain a sense of perspective. Simple breathing techniques like 7–11 breathing can help (breathe in for a count of 7, out for a count of 11, then repeat for a few minutes). Alternatively, try listening to confidence-boosting hypnotherapy or creative visualization downloads.

If you scored between 61 and 80 …

Stress sabotages your lifestyle

You may be surprised at how quickly stress can undermine your equilibrium, and disrupt your lifestyle balance. You may find yourself craving sweet stuff, eating erratically, relying on fast food or feeling hungry all the time. Then you start to skip exercise or yoga sessions, use wine to wind down, or spend evenings watching TV and snacking. Your weight, energy levels and how you feel about yourself then starts to yo-yo. Your big red flag is when you start to put off self-care activities because you 'don't have time'. That's your cue to do the opposite, and find more time for exercise, mindfulness, hobbies, cooking from scratch, reading or whatever you personally find sustains and nourishes you. Try setting yourself daily targets, like clocking up a certain amount of walking or meditation.

CHAPTER 3

HOW DOES REAL CALM *REALLY* FEEL?

W e'd like to give you an idea of how you can expect to feel so that you're clear about what you're aiming for. If you've been experiencing any kind of stress for a prolonged period of time, looking for the opposite of stress can feel like searching for keys, through the mud, in the dark, without even knowing which house is yours. We'd like to encourage you to think of finding ways to open up blinds and curtains and windows in the dark, stunning house that's you.

Your interpretation of the word calm and why you need to be experiencing this will now be clearer. Stress (wherever you're at in the continuum) is a chemical reaction in the brain, and deactivating this when it's not necessary, so you're not on constant alert, is the first stage. In Chapter 2 we clarified why you want to be calm and why you need to be calm. The challenges of life won't disappear but you will be better able to handle them, you will be in good health and you'll be flourishing rather than struggling.

In this chapter we want to take you through what happens in the body and the mind when you are calm.

YOU CAN ACCEPT ALL OF WHO YOU ARE

We've talked about that holiday feeling when you experience your best self and wish you could always feel like this, and we're encouraging you to look for ways to bring that Holiday-You into daily life. But of course in the daily grind of life, away from the stunning location and no demanding schedule, something else sets in: the aspects of you that you wish were 'better' or don't like.

We are lucky to live in a country and a society which values freedom and individuality, where people can live exactly as they please. The slight downside to this is that when there are no norms and there is so much choice people begin to question what they're achieving in a different way. Social media constantly reminds us of what others are doing. If there was only one norm, the natural tendency of human beings to compare ourselves and be competitive would be restricted to that one trajectory. When the norm was to get married at a certain age, have one job for life, have children, go on holiday once a year and do Christmas with the whole family, the natural tendency to compare and despair or compare and rebel was simpler.

But what now? Reality TV has made it possible to even be rich and famous without doing anything, and there are myriad images of what our lives might be and could be. What happens is that I *could* do this or I could do that becomes *should* I do this or should I do that multiplied several times.

And that creates anxiety. Add this to dealing with a stressful job and handling personal issues and you end up not feeling good about yourself. Some of you may even feel guilty because there's a lot of great stuff going on in your life, but you can't handle it all.

Real calm is about accepting where you're at along with all parts of yourself. It's about self-awareness rather than self-obsession. Self-awareness involves taking responsibility and certain actions – rather than staying stuck and hoping 'it' will all go away and falling into the trap of blaming others or feeling powerless. It's learning to shape your life so that life flows, rather than struggling to shape yourself into a life that aggravates you.

> **Many people are wondering – 'Is it all right to be me?' Because we are all too often encouraged not to be ourselves.**
>
> Jeremy Stockwell, performance consultant and TV coach

Right now you feel: Frustrated with yourself

Right now start: Telling yourself you're doing the best you can

ED HALLIWELL ON ACCEPTING YOUR STRESS AND ANXIETY

'The biggest challenge with focusing on the word calm is that it's not very helpful. It induces an expectation. There are so many ideas of what it is. We have to let go of what it is, what we imagine it to be, and to redefine it as competence: and that's the capacity to realize we can work with what's here.

American psychologist Carl Rogers said the paradox is that you can only change once you accept yourself, otherwise there is so much energy going into fighting what's here. And we have no choice in what's already here.

If you accept your stress and anxiety, and if you recognize this is not the whole of what's here, then you can train yourself to step out of this as a complete identification of you. This takes a lot of training. If we try to be calm in a bitty way from little tips and bits we will only be calm in a bitty way.

The more you tell yourself something is wrong and that you are not calm and should be calm, the more your stress is heightened.

We can't approach calm from trying. Trying to be calm is a false thing because it's a struggle. Struggle is the antithesis of calm. If we're fighting our situation and we're not calm, then calm means being with the difficulties and being with who we are.'

OTHERS EXPERIENCE YOU AS CALM

This section was originally entitled 'You look calm to others', but we dismissed this because it was misleading. It implies that you'd be faking confidence while others view you as calm. If you tend to be a nervous wreck in situations where you're in the spotlight, then *looking* calm might be at the forefront of your mind. You want to go into making a presentation or a pitch for business without looking nervous. Real calm, however, comes from the body. You don't *look* confident and calm, you *are* in control of the complex internal processes that kick off when you have to make a speech or pitch for business.

It's not that others see you as calm, but that they don't see you as anxious in any way. They might not describe you as calm because instead they might be inspired to describe you as knowledgeable, competent or even inspiring and dynamic. When others experience real calm from you they can experience the real you and the gems you have to offer.

Right now you feel: Nervous about the impression you make

Right now start: To reveal glimpses of the real you

CHARLIE WALKER-WISE ON WHY WE NEED TO RELEASE TENSION

'The Alexander Technique was developed by Frederick Matthias Alexander, who was a good friend of Sir Herbert Beerbohm Tree the founder of RADA, so RADA has a long relationship with this technique to release tension and operate optimally. The technique was created because Alexander himself was aware that when he got on stage he lost his voice and realized there must be something he was doing on stage that was responsible for physical strain. He created mirrors

to watch himself and realized that he was putting all sorts of tensions through his body. As a result he developed his technique to work with an engaged released body.

People say I want to control the room or I want to control my voice. Control suggests holding on. In fact it's about releasing tension so that sound resonates. In the context of sport, if you play golf or tennis you know you need to release your arm for a swing, you can't hold or overly control a swing.

So for effective communication we need to train the mind and body to work together to release tension. Tension is the enemy of communication and business is all about communication. We need to understand how we Think Breathe Speak (our motto for RADA in Business).

We have a thought, we take a breath. The breath is related to the thought we will communicate. If we see someone step out in front of a car and we know they are going to be hit we shout "LOOK OUT". But if a child gives us a picture drawn for us we say "aah, thank you so much". These two very clear breaths are very different.

The Latin word inspare, which means "breathe in", is the root of the word inspiration. We take different breaths according to the thoughts we want to communicate. The vagus nerve in the brain communicates thoughts to the diaphragm and tells the diaphragm to drop; an impulse is sent through the vagus nerve, with the brain saying: "you are going to communicate this thought now so please breathe in, we are about to speak". When it's a panic thought because we see the person is about to be hit by a car, it's a quick breath. When the child approaches with a picture for us and the thoughts are warm and fuzzy, we take time to take a longer, slower breath. So the body knows.'

LIFE LOOKS GOOD

When you are experiencing life through a stress filter nothing looks good, nothing measures up to how it 'should' be. As you know now from Chapter 2 the discrepancy monitor in the brain ramps up anxiety like a volume dial turned to full. Life isn't perfect, even for the rich and famous who seemingly have it all. Being able to see the good things you've created in your life and your achievements so far is one of the biggest benefits of real calm. In Chapter 1, one of the dimensions of our definition for real calm is striving rather than struggling in life, being able to flourish. When life looks good you can do this.

> **If you can just stop for a moment each day and sit without wanting, calm will come and find you. And gradually you will find you can extend these moments.**
>
> Jeremy Stockwell, performance consultant and TV coach

Right now you feel: Life isn't the way you want it to be

Right now start: Identifying just one thing a day that's good in your life

MIRIAM AKHTAR ON BUILDING POSITIVE EMOTIONS

'One of the functions of positive emotions is to neutralize the physiological effects of stress, including tensed muscles and raised blood pressure, and to dissolve the effects of negativity.

Calm is a positive emotion, but as an emotion it is not a permanent state. It's important to let go of the idea that emotions are permanent experiences. When you experience moments of calm, these are short-lived. Thinking you have to be permanently calm is stressful in itself.

People get hooked on the idea that it's possible to experience peak happiness all the time and then see themselves through that filter of needing it. There is a deep happiness that we can achieve through living a purpose, and there is happiness that is about peak moments of positive emotions. The more we accumulate calm moments, the happier we will feel. An anxious person is experiencing the opposite of calm. Calm is the antidote to endless looping thoughts.'

" A lot of people are spending a lot of time not feeling positive, compared to a moment of feeling better. "

Professor Ian Robertson, psychologist and neuroscientist

YOU'VE GOT YOUR MOJO BACK

Now what does this mean? Literally it means your magic charm. It's that spark that has you perform at your best, whether it's shining at work or making everyone laugh. Your mojo might also be passionate, opinionated, committed to campaigning for justice or the grit to achieve a competitive ambition like getting a thriller published or setting up your own business. Most of these don't exactly suggest calm do they? Some of these are up there with get-up-and-run-with-the-wolves or swim-with-the-sharks.

BREATHE TO 4-7-8

Health guru and *Psychologies* columnist Andrew Weil's 4-7-8 technique[1] is one that can easily be practised any time to relieve anxiety. He describes it as a natural tranquilizer and recommends practising twice a day:[2]

1. Exhale completely through your mouth, making a whoosh sound.

2. Close your mouth and inhale quietly through your nose to a mental count of **four**.

3. Hold your breath for a count of **seven**.

4. Exhale completely through your mouth, making a whoosh sound to a count of **eight**.

5. This is one breath. Now inhale again and repeat the cycle three more times for a total of four breaths.

Real calm is multidimensional and you will experience it in different ways. You'll be able to be fired up at work, but you'll also be able to switch off after work. When you see the neighbour you have an ongoing dispute with you'll be able to be detached and be polite, but when you join a local campaign to save a local business you won't hold back on telling the council your opinion. When there's a crisis in the family you won't wade into any arguments, but if someone in the family nags you you'll snap at them to respect you. There will be situations when you choose to be detached or cool – but this isn't what real calm is about on a more constant basis.

Detach-don't-react is common advice and certainly this applies in many situations. But it's not a mantra to live your life by. Real calm feels full of possibilities in terms of how you respond in any given situation. It's about being engaged in the moment, poised to unleash your mojo. Like driving a car, you're able to navigate traffic and tricky road conditions, speed up on the motorway when there's a clear run and slow down to take in breathtaking scenery.

Right now you feel: Constantly frazzled

Right now start: Pausing just for a few seconds

CHARLIE WALKER-WISE ON NEUTRALITY

'Neutrality is about being in a prime state to take action at any point, no matter what you're feeling. It's a concept that's big for us at RADA in Business. Connecting with neutrality is about finding the right balance between relaxation and tension. Calmness is great, but you can't be so calm you're floppy and de-energized, and of course you don't want excess tension as that is restrictive and a waste of energy.

In a professional context, emotion has a place and at times you have to step into that space of communicating with passion. You can't be detached. We often need to bring passion and fire to our work, and detachment suggests a disconnection. Neutrality means I am aware of myself, I am aware of what's around me. It's in this state that we perform at our best.

When people are with their friends they can be their most calm, centred selves. When we get into a professional context and we're dealing with all sorts of things we're not so familiar with, and the terms of reference are uncertain, then we come off our centre. We start getting tense.

*As soon as you are tense, it shows in your body and your
voice, and you stop connecting with your audience as
successfully. When this happens, the full power of your
message is lost. If we are tense, our breath is likely to be
high in our chest; this affects our voice and the impact
on our audience can be uncomfortable. We need to show
neutrality through our bodies.'*

Real calm might sound like it's a recipe for deep relaxation. While
there might be moments when real calm feels relaxing, that's not
the basis of it. Being able to accept how you are and focusing on
taking action to become competent at dealing with life problems
will help you avoid getting into the spiral of stress. Instead of
faking confidence and calmness you'll become aware of where
your body holds tension. The appreciation of the link between how
we think, breathe and speak will lead you to think more before you
speak. You'll be in charge of your responses, ready to ignite all of
your strengths when you need them.

REAL PEOPLE

"I discovered my calmness during a crisis" *– Jennifer*

'Stress wasn't just a part of my daily life, I believed that
was who I was and how I was. I blamed my awful periods,
boyfriends, work, family, everything and everyone. I couldn't
handle anything, everything was a drama, from charging
my phone and finding clean knickers, to a new demanding
boss. So when my father was diagnosed with cancer, you'd
have thought I'd be the last person to cope with this real

problem, especially with my mother not being well enough to look after him. I didn't hesitate to ask for unpaid leave to help my mother and be with my father. My older siblings had small children and couldn't do this, but I could and so I did.

I couldn't believe how calm I felt during some of the most painful times I ever experienced in my life. It was so weird. During these awful waits at the hospital, with no sleep for days, no proper food, and having to support my mum too, I never flapped. I couldn't. One night at the hospital my mum said to me "you can be ever so calm when you want to be". It dawned on me that being calm can be a personal decision. I could feel calm *and* in pain, calm *and* under pressure at the same time.

I did the gardening at my parent's house at first because dad couldn't do it anymore, and then because it made me feel better. Gardening became this soothing, calming escape.

I went back to work after seven months off, gutted that I'd lost my dad. Even though I lost him physically he's always there for me. I've stopped rushing around so much and trying to cram so many things into my life. I don't have a garden, but I've got the best window boxes and Juliette balcony, and I'm helping an elderly neighbour with her allotment. Gardening still clears my head and is soothing. It keeps me sane. If I start getting hyped up, I think about my dad and I slow down. I think of that person who was with him at the end, and that's the person I want to be all the time.'

ASK YOURSELF

Ⓠ Do you feel you should be calm? Why? Where did this 'should' come from?

Ⓠ Instead of calmness, how could you develop the skill of handling practical problems in your life? What skill could you learn that would help?

Ⓠ Forget calm for the moment. How negative do you feel about your life? What's good in your life?

Ⓠ What's positive about you not being calm? (Yes, really!) When is being fired up an advantage for you?

2 WHAT'S STOPPING YOU FROM FEELING CALM?

CHAPTER 4

WHAT'S AT THE ROOT OF YOUR STRESS?

ne of the most consistent voices in your head is likely to be a self-critical one: you wonder why you worry about even routine things like reading your meter for a utilities bill; you get angry with yourself for getting stressed about a family occasion that's entirely predictable; you feel inadequate for feeling stressed at work while your colleagues seem to be handling things fine; you feel guilty because actually life is pretty good, but you can't keep up.

So far we've looked at what it really means to be calm. Before we take a look at where you're at right now and the reasons you feel stressed, we're going to rewind to what's led up to now. It's difficult to deal with how you are at present while the headquarters of your brain have called the emergency fire engine and your head feels like an emergency siren. We've outlined that stress is a chemical reaction in the brain, but doubtless your question is: 'Yeah, but why can't I stop that happening?'

There are various factors which we'll address in this chapter. Whatever these factors are, stress has become your default setting. Once you become aware of why and how you can begin to reconfigure your responses.

YOUR EMOTIONAL EXPERIENCE SHAPES YOUR BRAIN

Let's start at the beginning. Whether you always remember feeling anxious as a child, or can pinpoint becoming anxious when there were cutbacks in your current workplace, how we experienced pressure in our earliest years plays a part in how we handle pressure as adults.

"Some people learn earlier on in life how to deal with life, maybe because of their parents, their school, their environment. We all have different starting points."

Ed Halliwell, mindfulness teacher and writer

We know from the pioneering work of psychoanalyst John Bowlby[1] that it's important for newborn babies to form a strong secure attachment to their mothers. 'If for whatever reason this doesn't happen,' says psychologist and neuroscientist, Professor Ian Robertson, 'this can lead to anxiety.'

From a neuroscience point of view, the brain of a newborn is affected when bonding with mummy doesn't happen (because mummy or baby are sick and separated for example). The amygdala (a key part of the brain responsible for emotion) displays differences when anxiety is rooted so early on. 'The amygdala is particularly active when people are anxious, and so, over many years, this leads to it becoming bigger because its networks of brain cells become more and more strongly connected with repeated use,' writes Professor Robertson in his latest book, *The Stress Test*.[2] In other words, it's like a muscle getting bigger and stronger with exercise.

Put in very simple language, anxiety might be more than a habit – it might be what your brain kicks into because it's *good* at being anxious. Viewing the brain as something like a muscle that can be trained and taking a neuroscience view can not only help you understand *why* you are the way you are, but it can fuel you with the motivation that it *is* possible to change. If you've always made soggy pasta until you taste real pasta on holiday in Italy, and the cook shows you how to cook it properly, well you won't look back.

"No human behaviour is untrainable or unchangeable – NONE."

Professor Ian Robertson, psychologist and neuroscientist

Our earliest experiences in dealing with uncertainty and problems become the recipes we follow as adults. We learn what to go for and what to avoid based on what we experience. If a teacher told you not to mumble the first time you read something out at assembly, you might have learnt to avoid speaking in public. If the whole school clapped enthusiastically and your teacher told you you're a natural, then making presentations might be one of your greatest strengths.

As human beings we fall into different behavioural modes based on how we feel. Psychologist Rob Gray[3] developed the theory of approach or avoidance. As Professor Robertson explains in his book, a key development in psychology came when Professor of Psychology and Psychiatry Richard Davidson[4] took Gray's approach/avoidance systems and applied these to emotional problems. People who are approach-based suffer less anxiety, while those operating more in avoidance mode experience low moods and anxiety. In terms of daily life this means that the more you want to avoid applying for a new job because you're not confident in interviews, or the more you avoid going to the GP because you're worried you might be seriously ill, the more you worry and this perpetuates a cycle. You continue to be anxious and this becomes a habit.

The great news is that it's possible to change.

Easier said than done: Stop worrying

Doable right now: Smile and give yourself a gold medal for worrying – and celebrate your new calm training

PROFESSOR ROBERTSON ON THE PSYCHOLOGICAL TRAITS WE INHERIT

'I don't believe it is possible to come up with a clear answer on heritability for most psychological traits. It depends on many variants, so the rule of thumb [between nature:nurture] is roughly 50:50. You can't do anything about your nature, your DNA. But there is huge research on nurture – the effect of upbringing, role models, decisions made, skills learnt, experiences, our overall environment. The human brain has so few genes and it's so plastic. Just 20,000 genes can't possibly code for the range of human behaviours.

We have evolved in order to be changed by our environment.

There are big influences in the environment. Even the psychology of identical twins is shaped by the particular experiences they have.

If you want to train someone to be a soldier or a pilot, then for sure you have to select your best suitable bets. But a huge amount of training then goes on.'

YOU'VE SOMEHOW KEPT A LID ON THINGS

It can be very confusing and unsettling to sense yourself out of control when you've prided yourself on dealing with challenges. You might wonder why you coped well in a far more demanding work environment several years ago or why suddenly you're a wreck. Even if you've always been a worrier, the worrying might not have got in the way in the past, but now it is. If you've somehow always kept going, without dwelling on the past and despite uncertainty about the future, why is *now* so difficult? And isn't soldiering on being resilient?

Things do add up. That's the nature of journeying through life and being human. You can keep painting over walls, creating the most flawless of rooms, but at some point you have to strip those walls bare and start again. Sometimes major life events trigger these seismic changes. A parent dies. A marriage breaks up. You lose your job. Your own business doesn't take off. You get seriously ill. You move. You move more than once in a year. Your flat is flooded and the ceiling falls through. Any major event can blast your usual coping modes out of the window and you find yourself lost in a backdrop of previous disappointments: all the heartbreaks, all the job disappointments, all the friendship betrayals, everything you soldiered through now haunts you. This is a painful place to be in, but it's normal and it will pass because you are addressing the problem.

Easier said than done: Move on from the past

Doable right now: Acknowledge and accept how you feel today

SANDRA ELSDON VIGON ON ANALYSING WHY YOU'RE AT WHERE YOU ARE

'When I begin the analytical process with a client, I start with where people are, and evaluate where they need to get to. I want to see who *is* there, what *is* there.

We are complex, multiple personalities. Everything that we cannot process falls into the unconscious. Nothing goes away; instead it's stored in the unconscious outside *time and space. But a crisis brings certain things to the surface. This is why people tend to seek therapy during a crisis. What comes up emotionally impels them to get help.*

It has to be determined whether what's coming up is old anxiety or an anxiety activated by circumstance. Everything in our psyche is interwoven. Where an emotion goes is not always obvious. Anxiety and trauma can come out in different ways including physical symptoms like skin and gut problems, or a deep depression might be triggered. Evaluating the symptom and getting to its root is important.'

YOU'RE HEADING FOR BURNOUT

When you stop to process your feelings and tackle emotional problems there's a risk of entering a relentless mental treadmill that eventually will wear you out. If you're working in an all-hours demanding work culture, are a workaholic, or for whatever reason have to take on more demands than you can handle (health issues plus problems with children plus work pressures, for example) anxiety is your mind's way of reminding you things are just too much.

Performance psychologist Dr Jim Loehr and Energy coach Tony Schwartz[7] have written about what we can learn from the relationship between emotions and energy in sports. There are four zones: performance, survival, relaxation and burnout, each with a different interaction between emotions and energy. In performance mode there is high energy and positive emotions, in survival mode there is high energy and negative emotions.

EMBRACE THE DANISH CONCEPT OF 'HYGGE'

According to the UN World Happiness League,[5] 33% of Danes feel calm, peaceful and happy – compared to 14% of Brits. Since Denmark consistently tops the happiness leagues (despite having similar grey weather) we can certainly learn from the Danish way of life. In the past year several books have been published on the Danish concept of 'hygge' (pronounced hue-gah) including one by Meik Wiking CEO of the Danish Happiness Research Institute.[6] The word literally translates as cosy but is more a philosophy about looking after ourselves. The Danes routinely ditch their smartphones and prioritize me-time, friends-time, family-time. If you're already a fan of Danish drama like *The Bridge*, *The Legacy*, *The Killing* and *Borgen* you'll already be feeling pro this Scandi culture. Hygge is all about candles, savouring cinnamon buns, baking, and snuggling by the fire. What's not to love?

Ideally we want to live our lives in the performance and relaxation zones – not survival and burnout. You know you're in performance mode when you thrive on challenges, you wake up excited and celebrate your achievements with fun downtime. If life feels relentless, however, and you're too tired to even sleep, that's a sign to step back and take action to restore yourself.

Easier said than done: Take on less

Doable right now: Take a moment to breathe now

MIRIAM AKHTAR ON UNDERSTANDING EMOTIONAL ENERGY

'Modern life seems to virtually exclude relaxation – and that's where calm is located. In organic farming there is a growing season and another when the field is left fallow to renew nutrients. We too need to renew ourselves.

Relaxation is a physical state. The autonomic nervous system has two branches – the "fight or flight" branch and the "rest and digest" one. For a calm mind we need to leave the everything-at-a-hundred-miles-an-hour state. We need to have our attention on one thing rather than multiple things, we need to be relaxing into yoga, instead of racing there, lying there thinking of what to do, and then ticking this off as relaxation. Calm is the antidote to endless looping thoughts and repetitive patterns of thought. It's located in relaxation. Relaxation is when you can switch off and be with the experience, it's about the state of being rather than doing. Society is very performance-focused and we want to keep doing. Yet we need time to digest our experience of being in the world.

We need to spend more time relaxing rather than performing. Going to a yoga class once a week for an hour simply isn't enough. In order to perform well we need to prioritize relaxation. We need to value time spent in the relaxation zone. Craft activities and baking have all made a come-back because people realize these activities are truly relaxing. They are "flow" experiences which put you "in the zone".

If we push ourselves beyond our limits, we're less able to experience positive emotions like calm. So much of our emotional psychological wellbeing is about coming into balance. When demands outweigh resources we need to reduce the demands. And that's hard to do.'

JEREMY STOCKWELL ON OUR ACHIEVE AND SUCCEED CULTURE

'There is the propensity in our culture to get everything right. Starting from our education system we fear getting things wrong because the education system is based on results. You have to achieve results at a certain time, you receive your pieces of paper that say you are smart, and on you go into the work environment where effectively you are stamped, filed, boxed and indexed. The corporate model is reductive rather than expansive. You keep going, thinking come the big day, things will be great. But you're always worrying.

You go through low-key everyday worry: there's the train to catch, there's what you have to cram into your day, and did you leave the gas on? Anxiety comes from many sources. You listen to radio or TV or look at news on your smartphone, receiving a stream of well-crafted news, so you worry about terrorism, what's happening globally, Brexit. Then there's all the information that makes you feel you have to be thinner, taller, wear this suit, these heels – and these are all very clever commercially inspired messages to make you believe you are not enough.

There's a coffee shop on every corner so you're buzzing with caffeine. You're fixating on Facebook and emails, wedded to the serotonin rush that occurs in the brain with the ping of a like or an email. Your life is contained in this little virtual world.

If you could switch off your phone, not look at the news, not watch TV, come away from that little virtual world, leave what you think you know, what passes as reality, you will allow yourself to experience a different reality, one that isn't based on achieving and succeeding.

*It's a curious thing that we feel we have to be achieving
and succeeding. Some people wake up at some point, often
around 40, and realize there's more to this thing. If they
are wise or fortunate they can bring about conditions in
themselves for change. Tuning in to calm is part of this.'*

YOU FEEL ANGRY, RESENTFUL OR REJECTED

These are three powerful emotions which may be causing you
additional feelings of guilt. And that's a hugely stressful situation
to be in. While researching this book, we came across leading
California-based anxiety specialist Reneau Z. Peurifoy's book,
Anxiety, Phobias and Panic (Piatkus), which was first published in
1988. A whole chapter in the book is devoted to feeling angry,
resentful or rejected. If you identify that these are emotions you
feel on a regular basis, it's a sign that your needs are not met.

Neuroscience confirms that bottling up emotions like anger affects
the brain and creates more stress. Professor Robertson writes[8]
that as human beings we have six basic emotions as part of our
evolutionary system: fear, surprise, happiness, sadness, disgust,
anger all play a part in our survival. 'Anger's role is at least partly
to get you what you want or need when your goal is thwarted.'

Professor Robertson explains in his book that if someone
criticizes us this switches on the left frontal lobe of the brain.
If there's no action, being upset turns into anxiety, which is
'unfinished business in the mind'. Answering back switches on the
right frontal lobe's approach–reward system. We do something. We
feel better. The problem is you can't shout back at your boss, you
can't blast your team and then expect to motivate them, and if you
answer back at friends consistently without processing whether
you're being sensitive or they have a point, you might not have any
friends left.

"I'm still training myself to be calm if someone speaks to me aggressively. I find it hard."

Professor Ian Robertson, psychologist and neuroscientist

The challenge is to cultivate what Professor Robertson refers to as 'constructive anger' – using the brain's approach energy to spell out clearly why you are angry and what you would like them to do about it. 'Suppressing emotions without reappraising them […] increases adrenaline-linked arousal responses, including raised heart rate, blood pressure and skin sweatiness. It also makes your memory poorer.'[9]

You might wonder how resentment and anger can be in the same category as rejection. If rejection is something you experience regularly, whether it's job rejection or social rejection, it may be reassuring for you in some way to know that the stress you feel as a result of rejection is not only real, it's serious. 'Rejection by others,' writes Professor Robertson[10] 'is the biggest stressor known to human kind and there are good reasons for this. In our evolutionary past, being rejected from the group meant you might be killed by enemies or predators. And social rejection makes us feel pain that switches on exactly the same brain networks as physical pain […].'

Whatever the negative emotion is, it won't go away easily. If you could snap out of it, you would. Enduring situations – like feeling angry with your neighbour who woke you up again, or feeling resentful someone less qualified and less experienced was promoted over you, or feeling rejected after yet another job application – is like being mentally battered. On a practical level what you need might be obvious: peace and quiet, promotion, a job. But your emotional needs may be more complex: to have people around you who value you as a good neighbour and are considerate to your needs, to be appreciated and valued for your contribution to the team, to have an identity you are proud of. Delving into your needs can help you focus on how to resolve your unmet needs, which in turn will take the lid off those simmering and boiling emotions.

> *Easier said than done: Get over your anger, resentment, rejection*
>
> *Doable right now: Ponder the* need *triggered by what you feel*

UNDERSTANDING WHY YOU'RE AT WHERE YOU ARE

We've delved into why you can't deal well with stress to give you a greater and gentler understanding of yourself so you can move forward without blaming yourself or others and without feeling guilty. Lodged in the recesses of your brain might be your earliest stressful experience: not being able to bond with mummy. And if your parents were experiencing difficult times, you wouldn't have been able to learn how to cope by mirroring them. Environment counts for half of our personality, so if you had a tricky time at school your coping skills won't have been developed – though the great news is it's never too late to learn these skills and change. There is *nothing*, our expert neuroscientist Professor Robertson confirms, that can't be changed if you put your mind to it.

There are times when circumstances in the present kick off a crisis, and that could be because of old wounds being triggered and coming up to be healed, or you might have taken on too much and are racing to burnout. If you're experiencing certain tricky-yucky emotions it's inevitable that these will keep your mind churning and miserable until you stop feeling guilty and focus on getting your needs met. Whatever the reasons for not being able to handle stress, these reasons are temporary.

"I'm not stressed – I'm a pushover" – *Alan*

'I've always been boiling with frustration, feeling stressed and unappreciated. I always seem to be sorting out other people's mess. My brothers can do no wrong, even though one never sticks to a job, and the other one is always getting into trouble. Being the oldest, I'm the one bailing them out with money or support, and still getting criticized by my parents. I work really long hours, cover for my boss, but get passed over for promotion. Plus my flatmates leave all the bills and landlord dealings to me. It's all very well being told I'm efficient, but what good does that do *me*?

I've become more and more stressed and it makes me unhappy because it feels like I'm a prisoner inside my brain. I keep hearing myself think things like: Life's unfair; if you're a good person you get stamped on. The few times I stood up for myself have been a disaster. Recently I was ill and couldn't organize our washing machine to be fixed. One of my flatmates got really annoyed and even said it was my job.

I think that's when the penny dropped – I'm not stressed, I'm a pushover. Did my flatmates help me out when I was sick? No. When I blew up, they were mortified and said they thought I was super capable and never realized I needed anything.

I've since decided to move out and live on my own. I'm also looking for a new job where I can make a fresh start. I'm reading a lot and investigating what I can do to learn to manage stress and look after myself by being more assertive. On a whim I signed up with a weight loss organization because the stress has just made me depressed and I've been stuffing my face with junk food, playing computer games and watching endless telly. It's turned out to be a great thing because it's as much about psychological support as what you eat, and I really need that. I'm determined to sort myself out and my dream is further along the line to train to help others like me.'

ASK YOURSELF

Q When you were a child, were your parents calm?

Q Does your anxiety date back to your childhood? Do you remember always feeling worried?

Q Is your desire to feel calm relatively new? What's the source of your stress right now?

Q How manageable is your life at the moment? Have you taken on too much?

Q Where in your life do you feel resentful or angry?

WHAT IS *REALLY* STRESSING YOU OUT?

Do you ever wonder why you take some situations in your stride, while other situations unsettle you and undermine your feelings of calm? It's not *what* happens to us that causes stress, it's the meaning we attach to it. By understanding the way your mind works, you can identify the unhelpful beliefs or thinking patterns that are distorting your perception of both the world around you, and your ability to cope with it. Sometimes, defences that we developed for good reason as we grew up can outlive their usefulness, and become a source of stress or low mood in themselves. Understanding how your mind works is the first step to changing it. Take this test to identify what's really triggering your stress, and what you need to do to change it.

Test by Sally Brown

QUESTION 1

The most stressful aspect of starting a new job is:

A. Not knowing what to expect on your first day.
B. Worrying that you will mess it up.
C. Ensuring you live up to your reputation.
D. Wondering if you will fit in and make friends.

QUESTION 2

A good friend forgets your birthday. What goes through your mind?

A. 'Maybe they're annoyed with me about something.'
B. 'There's no excuse for forgetting a good friend's birthday.'
C. A million things, from 'are they OK?', to 'has the post been stolen'?
D. 'Even my best friends aren't really that bothered about me.'

QUESTION 3

It's a good day at work when:

A. You get positive feedback on something you put a lot of effort into doing well.
B. You feel useful or that you're making a difference.
C. You do something inspiring or creative that captures your full attention.
D. You don't make mistakes and you get everything done.

QUESTION 4

A friend asks you to sign up for a challenging charity event. You would:

A. Say yes and immediately start training so you don't embarrass yourself.
B. Say yes, but feel tempted to pull out as the date gets closer.
C. Say yes, then later change your mind and say no, then change your mind again and say yes.
D. Only say yes if you could be sure you would do well at it.

QUESTION 5

Which strategy would you use to ensure you did well at something important to you?

A. Put in over and above what's expected in terms of work.
B. Question everything you've done, re-doing it several times.
C. Think and talk about little else until it's done.
D. Enlist the help of someone to help and advise you.

QUESTION 6

What keeps you awake at night?

A. Worrying about things that have happened in the past.
B. Worrying about what might happen in the future.
C. Worrying about what people really think of you.
D. Worrying about not coping and getting out of your depth.

QUESTION 7

Which affirmation do you find most calming?

A. 'I approve of myself and love myself deeply and completely.'
B. 'I feel joy and contentment in this moment right now.'
C. 'I accept myself and know I am worthy of great things in life.'
D. 'Every day in every way I am reaching my full potential.'

QUESTION 8

Growing up, you most wanted to:

A. Meet your parents' high expectations.
B. Avoid making mistakes and being criticized.
C. Believe that you were loved and approved of.
D. Feel safe and stop worrying.

QUESTION 9

You arrive at an important meeting, but realize you've forgotten your notes. You think:

A. 'Everyone will think I'm an idiot.'
B. 'That's so typical, I forget everything.'
C. 'How can I wing it so no one notices?'
D. 'I'm going to mess up the whole meeting.'

QUESTION 10

What do you see as your biggest barrier to calm?

A. An over-active mind that won't stop thinking.
B. Feeling constantly driven to achieve.
C. Feeling like you're never quite good enough.
D. Feeling you can't trust that people really like you.

Now, add up your scores from each answer using the following table, and read on to discover how your inner belief system is sabotaging your peace of mind.

	A	B	C	D
Q1	2	6	8	4
Q2	6	8	4	2
Q3	8	2	4	6
Q4	6	2	4	8
Q5	8	6	4	2
Q6	6	4	8	2
Q7	2	4	6	8
Q8	8	6	2	4
Q9	6	2	8	4
Q10	4	8	2	6

If you scored between 20 and 35 ...

Your source of stress is self-doubt

You may seem outwardly confident but can very quickly feel out of your depth, as you constantly question your abilities. When things are going well, you experience a blissful period of calm when you feel good about yourself. However, it only takes a minor argument with a partner, friend or work colleague for self-doubt to set in again, robbing your peace of mind. Your self-doubt can also colour your relationships, making you question whether people really do like you. It may be a feeling that you grew up with as a child, if you felt like an outsider, the least favourite sibling, or were bullied at school. You can't change the past or what other people think of you, but you can change your relationship with yourself. Start by asking yourself, 'how different would my life be if I decided today to accept and love myself for who I am?'

If you scored between 36 and 45 ...

Your source of stress is over-thinking

You are a creative thinker with a vivid imagination, but the flipside is you can conjure up convincing and detailed worst-case scenarios. As well as catastrophizing, you may also be prone to ruminating, and can get into toxic overthinking cycles. You may feel that you are 'working things out' with your overthinking, but you never seem to get to an answer. Depending on your mood, overthinking can take on a negative theme and become a mental review of past mistakes and everything that has gone wrong for you. It's no wonder calm feels so elusive for you. Your overthinking may have started as a defence against anxiety – if you can think through every eventuality, you can prepare for it – but it's now become the cause of your stress. Try limiting your worry time to 15 minutes at a specific time of day. When you slip into overthinking mode, mentally park it until 'worry time'.

If you scored between 46 and 60 …

Your source of stress is self-criticism

You live with a subtle but persistent inner critic, who is there to berate you on everything you do or don't do. Chances are you've got so used to this bullying that you don't even register it anymore. It may have been there since childhood – did you grow up with a critical parent who was quick to point out your failures, or who compared you unfavourably to a high-achieving sibling? You may have relied on your inner critic for motivation, berating yourself to 'get a grip' or 'stop being so pathetic' when life feels tough. But the bullying has long since ceased to be a positive force, and now simply wears you down and robs you of inner peace and calm. Compassion is the antidote to critical thinking – start to talk to yourself in the same way you would to a good friend. It's time to evict your inner critic and install a compassionate inner coach instead.

If you scored between 61 and 80 …

Your source of stress is perfectionism

You're focused and driven and want to reach your potential to live your best life. You set yourself the highest standards in whatever you do, whether it's baking a cake or writing a report at work, and it's no doubt got you far in life. But constantly striving to 'be the best' is sabotaging your sense of calm. Growing up, you may have got your parent's attention and approval by doing well, and that feeling of needing to be 'top of the class' has never left you. Are you aware of how much of your headspace and energy is consumed by your perfectionism, leaving you exhausted? You may have even turned your quest for calm into another achievement, and something to be 'good at'. It's time to reconnect with the joy of living, rather than simply ticking off achievements. Try experimenting with 'good enough' for a while – chances are, the only person who will notice the drop in standards is you.

CHAPTER 5

UNDERSTANDING YOUR MIND: WHEN TO SEEK HELP

W e've tackled what's at the root of your stress and what has led to it. In this chapter, we'll help you look at where you are right now in more detail so that you can decide whether you need extra support. This is necessary because when there has been an accumulation of pressurized periods, what can happen is that stress becomes the norm. Everybody complains about stress, so it becomes hard to know whether what you are going through is normal or not.

Establishing the extent and the effect of stress isn't straightforward. You need to be patient with yourself to identify the sources of stress and to separate these from the effects of stress on your body and mind. This can take a little time as you observe yourself. This means stepping back to monitor your moods, your reactions and responses, and how you feel physically in relation to what's happening at any given moment through the day and throughout the night (since disturbed sleep can indicate stress).

As you begin to do this you will notice patterns, which will help to indicate whether experiencing stress is connected to certain circumstances or whether you are experiencing a condition that has gone beyond stress. For example, do you wake up tired and anxious, get through the day with lots of caffeine but perk up when someone acknowledges you are a valuable part of the team? Then perhaps you thrive on a certain type of challenge and need to find a way to change your lifestyle to support you.

On the other hand, if you are constantly on a roller-coaster of defensive explosions and weepy outbursts, lifestyle changes like giving up coffee and going to yoga may not be enough to help you recover. This chapter will give you a sense of where you are.

ASSESS YOURSELF

It's not unusual for people to be unaware of how stressed they are until they visit their doctor about a health issue that seems unrelated to stress. So how do you know what's normal? When should you worry? This is where you need to learn to monitor yourself. The chemistry of stress stops the brain from being objective, so if you are experiencing chronic stress your mind might be on autopilot. Assessing yourself isn't as clinical as it sounds. Think in terms of being curious about you and how you live your life. Then this becomes a rewarding process that is bound to lead to taking action.

There are various ways to assess yourself. The NHS has a free online Mood Self-Assessment questionnaire.[1] Depending on the results, your GP can go through a more detailed version to help you identify whether the problem is veering towards depression, anxiety or a mixture. Tracking your mind is a big part of cognitive behavioural therapy, which is based on changing your mood through changing your thoughts and behaviour. When you're stressed, the very idea of tracking your mind can seem overwhelming and unattractive. A very simple modified version is to score yourself daily for positive moods on a scale of 1–10 and include a minus 1–10 scale too. Depending on where your daily score is on the positive 1–10 scale you can assess the level of action you need to take on your own. But if you start to see a pattern of minus scores, or consistent 1–3s, then this is a definite sign to seek help.

Another (or additional) way is to take a more creative approach. Jungian psychotherapist Sandra Elsdon Vigon encourages describing your emotional state with imagery. 'Ask yourself what does this feeling look like? Is it pecking at you like a bird? Is it biting you? If it was an animal what would it look like?' etc. Engaging your feelings in a visual way can help you gain a deeper understanding of the nature of your stress. Vigon often asks clients to draw how they feel or create collages.

> ❝ **Many people get stuck on labels about what ails them, but what's important is to explore what's at the core of your unique experience.** ❞
>
> Sandra Elsdon Vigon, Jungian psychotherapist

Remember that stress interferes with the brain's ability to be objective and rational, so what happens is that you get into the pattern of believing you're stressed because of your job or because of a relationship. It's normal to be upset about a boss who doesn't value you, or a relationship that's ending. That is part of life. As you become curious about your life and investigate, what will become apparent is why you are *constantly* upset, worn out and unable to enjoy life. The important thing, as Vigon stresses, 'is heeding the messages' that your body and unconscious are sending. Feeling low should not be the norm.

ED HALLIWELL ON MAKING SPACE IN THE MIND TO UNRAVEL HOW WE FEEL

'It can help to name what's going on. Labelling our experience can help ground us. This is part of mindfulness training. Recognizing stress and noticing anxiety without totally identifying with these states helps us avoid getting completely caught up in them. As soon as you notice a state, you are stepping out of being it.

Noticing is different to constantly thinking you are one state or another. The process mustn't be self-involved so that you are not trapped in those experiences. It's the difference between "oh God, I'm so anxious" and noticing "ah, right, there's some anxiety there". This is a kinder way of experiencing so that we are not caught in the experience feeling this is who I am.

This process trains us to stay present and centred, in T.S. Eliott's words, to be "the still point of the turning world". There may be circumstances we can't control or that we don't like, but we can influence our attitude.

The more we train to do this, the more we can work with the external circumstances. It's about looking for possibilities where we have space to be still and calm. If we don't have the option to make a different choice, like find a different job, we can consider other options – can we go out for lunch instead of eating at our desk? Can we find other people to connect with for mutual support?

The reality is that we can't have everything we would like to have. Mindfulness trains us to let go of the magic quick fix. We can begin to work with our inner and outer experiences so that we move towards ways of managing things more helpfully. Mindfulness trains us to let go of the magic quick fix.'

SEPARATE NORMAL FROM EXCESSIVE

One of the problems in the current economic and political climate is knowing what's normal and what's excessive in terms of any negative emotion about the future. Creating a successful life on all levels involves navigating realistic concerns. However, when does realistic become pessimistic?

There will be times when uncertainty in the world ignites a tendency for anxiety. This is human. Jungian psychotherapist Sandra Elsdon Vigon admits she wasn't immune to massive anxiety in 2008 when the recession hit the USA and she and her artist husband lost their retirement income in California. As a result they had to move to the uncertainty of creating a new life in London. Learning to separate normal concerns from excessive worry and anxiety is a valuable modern skill. A key question to ask yourself is whether there is evidence for what you feel so that you can identify whether it's your circumstances causing you stress (e.g. a critical boss or partner) or your belief systems (e.g. lack of self-worth and confidence). This simple question can help you identify what course of action to take next (e.g. to deal with source of stress and how you respond to this or tackle reformulating your belief system).

It's normal to worry about specific issues, but when this turns into consuming fear about life at large then this has become a serious anxiety condition. As you now know, stress over something you perceive as a threat triggers a chemical reaction in your brain. With anxiety you are suffering from the onslaught of constant chemical warfare in your brain. Anxiety can develop as a result of stress or worries piling up – or both. Worry has a nasty habit of distracting you so that you don't even realize the extent of mounting stress. This is why you need to actively step out of whatever mode you are in to observe the degree to which it's affecting your ability to be fulfilled in life. Remember, real calm is a life that satisfies you.

JEREMY STOCKWELL ON ESCAPING FROM WORRY

'People usually have a good reason for worrying – work results, exam results, relationships, money – or they are predisposed to worry because of the way they were brought up, or due to incidents and accidents.

The Buddhists say that the mind is like a mad monkey. Thinking of all the things we could have done, should have done, or will do, prevents us from being in the here and now. Our job is to still that monkey. But if we strive to do this and it doesn't work, we get frustrated. The more you try to rid yourself of your thoughts, the more ripples you make in the process. By the same principle, does it work when you try to love someone? When a child tries to be good? By dint of trying you create nervous anxiety and that stops you being calm in any scenario.

Once a day, just for a little while, to be calm it can be very useful to stop, get out of your mind and come to your senses through your body. You can just sit quietly in your chair listening to the birds sing. Or you can go for a walk, stroke the cat, play Frisbee, put some music on and dance, or do anything that gets you out of your mind. It's quite simple when you allow yourself the time.'

WHAT'S YOUR LIMIT?

Real calm varies from person to person. We're all different compositions in terms of hormones and psychological make-up. You might marvel at the friend who gets up and makes speeches at weddings and has everybody laughing, because you break out in a sweat at the thought of any public speaking. But that friend might be in awe of you for being brave enough to try new evening classes on your own. Stress lies in the eyes of the beholder.

As part of being curious about yourself, explore when you come to your limits – and why. It's all too easy to keep lumping stress in one same basket, as if stress is stress. There are many variations. If your psychological make-up is high on the introvert scale, then a job in which you are constantly interacting with big groups of people is going to be more stressful and leave you feeling drained and exhausted. Becoming aware of this can help you find work where you thrive and feel energized. If you observe that you're over-reacting to everyday situations, there might be a hormonal issue, which is something you need to discuss with your doctor. There could be a physiological explanation to your moods that can be remedied with help.

TAKE A HOLIDAY FOR SIX DAYS

A recent study[2] took a group of women aged 30–60 to the same holiday resort for six days, with half of them randomly selected to join a meditation training programme, the other half simply enjoying the resort, plus an additional group experienced in meditation taking the meditation classes. The scientists from the Icahn School of Medicine at Mount Sinai, the University of California and Harvard Medical School measured stress levels before, and one month and ten months after the holiday. They found that not only did the holiday reduce stress levels, this lasted post-holiday. For the meditating groups the benefits lasted longer, in particular the experience meditation group. What's significant about this test is that as well as looking at what participants reported, it also measured the molecular network patterns in their brains for an accurate biological measure of the body and the immune system. The study concluded that meditation changes how our bodies function and can lead to healthy ageing. Whether you meditate or not, however, a six-day holiday will have lasting benefits.

Knowing yourself on every level, from psychological to physiological, can help you create a stress-ability profile. Know what you can handle, under which circumstances, for how much time, and you are prepared. An awareness of how you react under certain circumstances can at least prepare you. Jungian psychotherapist Sandra Vigon says that knowing she has a tendency to be hysterical under immense stress helps her handle the hysteria because it doesn't take her by surprise.

Most importantly in the context of this chapter, being clear about what you can handle, your limits and how you react gives you a map that tells you when you need nurturing and nourishing.

PROFESSOR ROBERTSON ON HOW TO APPROACH CALM FROM DIFFERENT STATES OF MIND

'There are different ways to approach calm depending on the psychological state.

Depression is loss of pleasure from anything. It's a feeling of hopelessness and a pessimism about future. Depression affects the hippocampus part of the brain, so memory is affected.

An anxious person is worried, but is not necessarily incapable of experiencing pleasure.

In both cases there are negative beliefs. For the depressed person they are: I am no use, there is no point, nothing will get better anyway. These faulty beliefs contribute to depressing emotions further. CBT (cognitive behavioural therapy) is needed to change these beliefs. In depression the focus needs to be on the behaviour, not just the cognitive side. There's an emotional deadness with depression, so for a therapist it's about getting people to engage in situations where they experience a feeling of pleasure as this switches on the reward mechanism of the brain.

With anxiety the content of the negative beliefs is different. It's about the downside of the future. Here a therapist's task is to get people not to avoid situations they fear and to take actions to confound their worst fears of what might happen.

Bipolar disorder, where there is true oscillation between manic highs and lows, and schizophrenia are classifiable as medical. But everything else is on a continuum. When it comes to disorders of mood and anxiety there may be genetic factors, but in terms of what to do there are optimal ways in terms of behaviours, decisions, interactions that are major determinants in change. Change is possible.

We have this capacity with the brain to live in different time zones. We can be anxious and find the future threatening or we can be depressed in the past world. But if we remember very simple tricks we can bring our minds out of these envelopes of time into the present. Just by breathing, expanding our posture, saying I am excited, we can do that. Calm is about keeping your attention on the moment, not what's happening next or what happened in the past.'

WHEN YOU HIT ROCK BOTTOM – THE ONLY WAY IS UP

Much of the advice in this book is about learning to be in the present. But what if you're feeling that there's absolutely no power to your now because now doesn't feel good? What if you're fed up with a cycle of bad experiences and a never ending awful present? If you're at the point of simply functioning in life on autopilot in order to get by from day to day, this isn't a good place to say the least. To restore yourself you need to be kind to yourself so that you can then experience life in a kind way. When you feel like this it's virtually impossible to climb out of this pit on your own.

Unless you take action you find yourself moving further along the continuum of stress. The end station to that continuum can be depression, burnout, or a breakdown of some sort

> ❝We live in a culture where people wear their stress as a badge of honour.❞
> Miriam Akhtar, positive psychologist

A significant report last year[3] (2016) warned that chronic stress and anxiety lead to a higher risk of developing depression and dementia because of the effect on the way the brain operates. The Rotman Research Institute's review looked at studies that had investigated the impact of chronic anxiety, fear and stress in animals and humans. Though stress is natural before and during certain events, like exams or public speaking, when it becomes a 'pathological state' the body's immune, metabolic and cardiovascular systems suffer, the brain's hippocampus degenerates, and this can lead to neuropsychiatric disorders. Thankfully the good news is that stress-induced damage to the brain is *not* irreversible. If you are reading this having hit rock bottom, there certainly is a way up.

When you are at this level it's important to be compassionate towards yourself and recognize that you are paralysed. Would you expect yourself to recover from a major injury without help from surgery, rehabilitations, friends and family rallying round to give you practical and emotional support? Emotional paralysis can be healed, but also requires specialist help. This could be counselling, psychotherapy, CBT (cognitive behavioural therapy), life coaching, healing – thankfully there are many options for you to choose from to suit you. A prolonged period of minus satisfaction in your life leaves you not knowing what to do – and that alone is a reason to seek structured help.

Recovering from a crisis can become a pivotal time in your life for making major changes so that you come out of this terrible period wiser, stronger and resolved to live the life that you deserve.

"Depression is like a negative form of calm: people have gone past anxiety, the world is overwhelming and they are exhausted, so they shut down in an unhealthy way."

Miriam Akhtar, positive psychologist

SANDRA ELSDON VIGON ON RECOVERING FROM A MAJOR CRISIS

'When we experience a major crisis we take a big hit. Our emotional foundations are shaken. We need to give ourselves time to recover. During this period one needs support and help to reconstitute and recalibrate the self.

In the workplace, redundancy can be a major blow. People can experience their identity being stripped away. Any such job loss can feel like the rug has been pulled from underneath and can strip you bare. Innate vulnerabilities that might not have been obvious before can surface at these times.

Some people are able to deal with such dramatic events calmly and experience anxiety after the event. There is a part of the brain that kicks into survival mode during crisis, a necessary ability to respond in the moment. Then, sometime *afterwards, the shock of the trauma hits. All trauma has to be processed. We are not robots. If it's not processed it will come out in other ways or stay lodged in our psyche.*

There are some people who are fearless no matter what happens. But they are rare. Most of us are not like this.'

Putting the pause button on your racing mind to work out why it's racing and where it's racing to is a crucial step to finding real calm. When you're used to having to keep moving, your motor is constantly running and you have to keep going. But just as every car needs and is required to have an MOT, our internal Ministry Of emotional Transport needs to get checked out too. And it's only when we stop to examine what's going on that this is possible. You might be so frazzled you're not even aware until you stop to observe your thoughts what it is exactly you feel. And what you feel is not you – it's a temporary state that can change. Whether you're worrying about every detail in your life or anxious about your future, whether you're mentally and physically exhausted with stress or stress has beaten you into depression, taking the mental steps to observe, acknowledge and process is a move towards the road sign that says real calm.

Stepping back to assess yourself is the first step to affirming that you are taking action to solve the problem of stress. Observing your moods from day to day and even within the day can give you valuable clues. As you unravel your thoughts and emotions a pattern will emerge that will enable you to decide how much stress is running your life. If you are past your limits and stress is ruining your health and ability to enjoy life then it's time to seek help. Depending on the effect stress has had on your mind, there are different approaches to healing yourself. Recovering from a crisis following a long period of an accumulation of stress certainly isn't easy – but it can be a time for developing a regenerated you.

"I gave up a great salary for a stress-free life" – Claire

'I don't know why I wanted to manage a sales team when I found selling terrifying. I was motivated by earning an amazing salary and having a great sounding title. The company I worked for had amazing incentives like gourmet weekends and spa trips in exotic locations. I loved the money and the lifestyle. I was stressed all the time with work but assumed this was normal. I would rather have worked in public relations but I turned down a job that came to me because it wasn't well paid.

So I drank more, binged and then went on diets and punished myself in the gym to cope with the stress. The turning point was getting ill. I was constantly ill. My company was supportive but I was trying to work from home and keep up with everything at work while I was ill. There was a takeover, job cuts, and I was terrified, especially as I didn't rate myself. I went back to work but I wasn't 100%. I would put on a front, then just go home and crash in front of the TV and sleep a lot at weekends.

Ironically it was at a fancy spa on a detox that I had a wake-up call. A doctor supervising the detox asked me if I enjoyed my job and my daily life. I didn't answer. He gave me a pep talk for which I am grateful. I cried most of the week.

I got back to work and, without planning it, I resigned, with absolutely no idea what to do next. The company offered me sick leave and I said no. They offered me a sabbatical part-paid I said no. Of course I was worried about the money and what to do next, but I was so relieved to leave that this outweighed the worry.

Most of all I didn't want to be sick with no energy, I wanted to recover. I'd had all sorts of problems with my house – leaks and floods and boilers and break-ins. I put it on the market and took the first offer. I sold most of my belongings and anything left I gave to charity shops. I didn't care about money any more, I wanted to be happy. I moved back to my home town and now run a small business organizing events. I earn less money – but I don't need to spend as much. It's a different kind of stress. I enjoy the challenge. Calm for me is being able to be me and not put on a front or worry what other people are saying about me.'

ASK YOURSELF

Q Without thinking about the question, give a number: what percentage of your day is stressful?

Q Are you worrying about one particular situation or several?

Q When was the last time you weren't worried, anxious, stressed?

Q Are you surviving your life, getting by, or living it?

HOW DO YOU HANDLE STRESS?

The stress response is hard-wired into our limbic system, the oldest part of our brain designed to keep us alive. And when we feel under threat, we still react in the same three ways as our early ancestors – fight (using attack as a form of defence), flight (running away from feelings and problems) or freeze (withdrawing or pretending nothing's happening). Uncovering your instinctive, default response to feeling threatened will help you identify the most effective way to soothe and nurture yourself when you're under pressure.

Test by Sally Brown

QUESTION 1

When you were told off as a child, you'd be most likely to:

A. Have a huge tantrum.
B. Threaten to leave home.
C. Burst into tears then sulk.

QUESTION 2

When you get into a heated argument at work, you:

A. Find it really hard not to cry.
B. Say a lot of things you later regret.
C. Want to walk out and not come back.

QUESTION 3

When you're really upset, you:

A. Feel too churned up to eat.
B. Either completely lose your appetite or feel extra hungry.
C. Use food and drink to escape from your feelings.

QUESTION 4

Drinking too much tends to make you:

A. Go quiet and reflective.
B. Talk and argue more.
C. Act on impulse.

QUESTION 5

You and your partner can't agree what to watch on TV. Your response is to:

A. Keep debating it until you get your way or find a compromise.
B. Let your partner choose, then watch while texting or reading emails.
C. Suggest you do something different instead like go out.

QUESTION 6

You find out some close friends are meeting up and they haven't invited you. You're most likely to:

A. Keep them at arms' length for a while and see other people.
B. Get it out in open, semi-joking about being left out.
C. Pretend you're completely fine with it, while feeling hurt and confused.

QUESTION 7

You've been given a tricky project to do at work that you can't seem to get started on. You end up:

A. Feeling angry that you've been landed with it and let everyone know about it.
B. Leaving it to the last minute, then finishing it overnight in a tearful panic.
C. Doing it at the last minute, while fantasizing about leaving your job.

QUESTION 8

When you're going through a tough time, your ideal weekend would be spent:

A. On the sofa with a box set.
B. Getting away somewhere, even just for a day trip.
C. Meeting up with someone you can offload to.

Now, add up your scores from each answer using the following table, and read on to discover the best way to soothe your instinctive response to stress.

	A	B	C
Q1	4	6	2
Q2	2	4	6
Q3	4	2	6
Q4	2	6	4
Q5	4	2	6
Q6	6	4	2
Q7	4	2	6
Q8	2	6	4

If you scored between 16 and 26 …

You react to stress by freezing

Stressful situations can make you feel paralysed. Your normal logical thinking processes shut down, so you can't rationalize and lose your sense of perspective. Even simple decisions begin to feel impossible. When you go into freeze mode, your basic instincts are telling you to crawl into your cave, so don't be surprised if you feel exhausted, no matter how much sleep you get, and find yourself withdrawing socially and avoiding conversations. If you're a procrastinator who tends to put off difficult situations until the last minute, chances are your default response to stress is freeze mode. Introverts tend to revert to freeze more than extraverts, by internalizing feelings and emotions – you might seem outwardly calm, but your stress manifests in other ways, like insomnia, eczema, IBS or low mood. To you, pulling up the drawbridge and relying on yourself rather than other people feels safest when you're under threat. But the best way to soothe yourself when you're in freeze mode is to reach out and ask for help. When your brain is in lock-down, you need someone else to help you process the situation and regain a sense of perspective. If there is one change you can make in your life right now to take you nearer to calm, it's to open up and talk more – fight against your urge to shut down, and let people know when you're struggling.

If you scored between 28 and 38 …

You react to stress by fighting

The first sign that your equilibrium is out of balance and you have lost touch with your sense of calm is that you're permanently on the defensive. You see criticism and personal attacks where none were intended. You may even rehearse angry speeches in your head so you feel prepared for attacks that you're sure are inevitable. Initially, it can become an energizing force, galvanizing you into action and defending yourself. But spend too much time in 'fight' mode and eventually, everyone seems like the enemy and you begin to create conflict where there is none. Eventually, operating in fight mode depletes you of energy, so even when you're arguing, your anger can quickly turn to tears. Breathing exercises are an essential 'first-aid' for you, and a surprisingly powerful way of calming the fight response because it engages the parasympathetic nervous system – try breathing in for a count of four, pausing for a count of four, then breathing out for four. Make time throughout the day to do this for three or four minutes. The more often you do it, the more effective it will be when you need it most. It's also important to prioritize some form of exercise every day, to help your body process the excess adrenaline that is fueling your aggression.

If you scored between 40 and 48 ...

You react to stress by flight

If you often feel trapped or backed into a corner, there's a good chance that flight is your default stress response. If you can't physically remove yourself from a threatening situation, you do it emotionally, by dissociating or creating an invisible barrier around yourself. When you feel under pressure, you often wrongly assume that a situation or relationship is irreparable and that quitting, giving up or leaving is your only option. You may also have a tendency to jump the gun, bailing out of a relationship or job because you've become convinced it's only a matter of time before you get dumped. You're in flight mode when you start to push people away or self-sabotage by behaving badly. People who default to the flight response when stressed can be mistaken for being unreliable or flaky. When you're craving freedom, you can go into 'all or nothing' thinking mode, and feel convinced that the only solution to how you feel is jacking everything in and going to live in a beach hut in India. Ask yourself: 'What evidence is there that running away is my only option?' Remind yourself that all emotions are transient, and you won't feel like this forever. And don't underestimate the soothing effects of smaller hits of freedom, like taking a few days off and going for long, rambling, soul-soothing walks in green places.

CHAPTER 6

STRESS
TRIGGERS

Y ou've now gained an understanding of why you're not calm. This understanding in itself can help you ease yourself out of your mind's current cage. You're aware that stress triggers a chemical reaction and that this is what humans are wired up to experience, and that the key lies in identifying the point at which stress catapults you into an unpleasant state of feeling. In this chapter we're going to identify the most common traps you can fall into that stop you from experiencing calmness. These stress triggers are major obstacles on your road to calm.

Some of these triggers won't surprise you in the least. Other triggers are likely to make you stop and think because they could be issues you haven't considered before. If the odd one sparks a big resistance, don't worry. Take your time to review it and approach it from different directions. You might even discuss it with friends who are going through a similar experience.

1. IGNORING YOUR NATURE

Whether you are an extrovert or an introvert (or an ambivert somewhere inbetween), be aware of how this influences your energy. There is no point in wishing that you could be better at being on your own or that you could enjoy networking and parties. It's pointless wishing you could be like your more confident, outgoing work self outside work or vice versa. All of this is negative thinking that creates stress. Instead of labelling yourself as one type or another, and rather than forcing yourself into situations you find stressful, consider what you need to be at your best.

This doesn't just apply to how you are with people around you. It's equally valid for the dynamics you find yourself in with others. If you're someone who likes to be helpful but then feels overwhelmed with demands, then you need to figure out when to say no, and how. Again, it comes back to what is your sweet spot or what is your tipping point. It can be helpful to not only identify your strengths but to also consider the perimeters of these. Your strength might be efficiency, but what do you need to be efficient? (Enough time? A competent team?) What affects your efficiency in a negative way and what boosts your efficiency? Similarly, in areas where you are not naturally strong, how does covering up for this make you defensive and stressed? What do you need to boost this area (like more support from your manager or partner)?

As we saw in Chapter 5, knowing yourself is the foundation to finding a calm you. So it's vital not to ignore You.

What do you need to remember about yourself?

What's the one thing you can do to boost rather than drain you?

2. CRITICAL VOICES

There you are, doing your best, and there's always someone telling you that you're not trying hard enough or you're not going about life correctly. You might have well-meaning parents or siblings who don't realize they are being critical, friendships where there's an unhealthy dynamic (they know best, always), and difficult colleagues and bosses. We'll hazard a guess that whoever is telling you to calm down is contributing to your stress, and even labelling you as critical if you try to assert yourself. Yep, we thought so.

> " **Somebody telling you to calm down or stop worrying can make you feel much more stressed. It can't be magic-ed.** "
>
> Ed Halliwell, mindfulness teacher and writer

The problem is that critical people seem to be everywhere in your life, right? And life's hard enough; you begin to doubt yourself and feel worse. So long as critical people feed on *your* self-criticism, you can't be calm.

One of the by-products of being self-critical is that you may be interpreting others as critical when they may be something else. If you can pause and consider whether the other person is engaging with you in a certain way because they are stressed, or whether they're not terribly sensitive to how sensitive you are, you might change your perspective and help avoid being triggered.

Now that you're on the process of unravelling how you feel, you'll be able to accurately pinpoint not only *when* you least feel calm but also *who with*. Just by reminding yourself that someone, whether they are a boss or a date, makes you feel criticized will be illuminating. This marks the beginning of you being gentle with yourself.

You can't change your boss, but you can say no to another date. If you know certain people are likely to criticize you, you can prepare to handle this predictable situation in whatever way works best – a ready line asking them to stop, ignoring the comment, getting up and going to the toilet.

Dealing with critical people starts with looking after yourself and developing self-compassion, because the biggest critic of you is likely to be you.

> " **People need help to change an emotional default setting based on criticism and judgement. This is a gradual process of creating a new healthier version to replace the negative pathways and structures.** "
>
> Sandra Elsdon Vigon, Jungian psychotherapist

Who is guaranteed to send you over the edge?

What could be one sentence that provides a buffer for you?

ED HALLIWELL ON SELF-COMPASSION

'We need to be gentle with ourselves, and for this we need self-compassion.

The way we've evolved to manage threat is such that we don't naturally click into a gentle voice when we feel stressed. In evolutionary terms, there's a certain urgency when faced with a wild animal to get out of the way. This isn't the time to speak to ourselves in a soothing manner as that doesn't help us in a dangerous situation when we have to move fast.

Tensing up and being on high alert is sensible when faced with a wild animal. Some voices are designed to help us survive. Even our critical voices are trying to help in some way, and we can be compassionate with them, even though they're not helpful. But these voices aren't always appropriate when the issues aren't about survival.

You can train yourself to not buy into the voices: I'm not currently faced with a bus coming at me – I'm faced with a problem in my life I can't run away from or fix quickly.

Automatic thoughts that come up are designed for different situations. If we can recognize these different situations, then that's the beginning of self-compassion. When you hear that voice, do recognize it but don't try to fight it or push it out. This is the beginning of self-compassion.

It takes training and work to do this, but if we think about how we've evolved over millions of years, we can't just click out of it. Recognizing this is self-compassionate.

> *The wonderful thing is we are as human beings capable of awareness. It's possible to step out of our automatic thoughts and feelings. We can see them rather than be in them. Mindfulness trains us to learn how to unhook from those automatic responses and work with them in a more skillful, compassionate way.'*

3. YOUR EGO

If your identity comes from standing out in any way, this one's a real biggie. Part of the reason your calm self is elusive might be because your busy self is the one who shines. Friends might admire your lifestyle, family might be proud of your status and all that you've achieved, you might even have dependents you feel responsible for, so how could you possibly stop?

You might have been able to sustain a certain lifestyle that once upon a time excited you, and now letting it go is hard. You might not have achieved your dreams and be determined to stick out the process, because that's resilience and grit isn't it? If you're craving calm then there's something not right about your process of living. By reading a book like this you are certainly facing up to it.

> ## " Busyness can be addictive and habitual. There's a sense of a void when you stop. What do you do now if you're not busy? "
>
> Professor Ian Robertson, psychologist and neuroscientist

What are you bent on achieving no matter what?

How can you spend more time on one thing that's flowing in your life?

JEREMY STOCKWELL ON SELF-ILLUSION

'If we create an illusion of self which is based on wanting people to think we are clever and smart then we are in a permanent state of agitation. If you easily snap to defend yourself and what you know, this belies insecurity – and insecurity creates anxiety.

Belief is from the old English word lief *which means wish. We be-wish the world the way we want to see it, so we get into "you are wrong and I am right". The opposite of be-wish is faith. Faith is saying to yourself: "I don't know. But I'm just going to trust." In a fast changing world with so many options and opinions coming at us 24/7 we need faith more than ever these days – whether that's a religion, a spiritual connection, ecological awareness, or a delight in nature. It's important to come home to yourself once in a while. We all need somewhere to moor our boat.*

If every day, just for a moment, we practise coming back to reality and actuality, then nerves and anxiety will reduce, or vanish altogether, and we will soon develop inner calm. It won't happen overnight. You will need to be diligent about it and practise for a little while very day.'

4. SETTING CALM AS THE GOAL

You probably sense this already. Why can't you 'just' calm down when things get to you? Why can't you *be* calm instead of stressed? Now you've got the key message in this book that it's a chemical reaction in your brain, you know that 'just' calming down is like trying to unboil a kettle of water. The water needs time to cool down.

> ❝ **If you make calm the goal, you'll screw it. Because then you will try to hold it. When you try to control, you tense up physically.** ❞
>
> Jeremy Stockwell, performance consultant and TV coach

In Chapter 2 we talked about why you want to be calm and why you need to be calm, so reviewing these points will help you identify what it is you really need.

Which situations have you screaming inside to calm down?

What's an alternative to aim for?

ED HALLIWELL ON REFRAMING HOW WE FEEL

'We can't magic calm. We need to find other ways to induce a deeper calm that can coexist with anxiety.

We have these experiences which physically feel unpleasant, like feeling our stomach churning and our heart beating faster. Our immediate interpretation is that a bad thing is happening, I shouldn't be feeling this.

But you can try instead to see what's happening as interesting and useful: My body is alerting me to something; it's trying to help me identify a perceived threat and is giving me information I need to find a way to work with this.

You can then shift to thanking your stomach and palpitations for alerting you. This mental shift has a whole different feel *to: this is awful, I'm anxious again, it's all going wrong, I won't be able to handle this, I can't cope.*

We can't force ourselves into a particular state. But reframing what we are experiencing gives us a mental space to recognize what's happening, and the possibility to ground and work with sensations.

Setting out to be calm can turn into a fight with ourselves and this becomes a way of beating ourselves up when we can't achieve this. Calm isn't something we can click into.'

5. A WANDERING MIND

We all thrive on being alert in every situation. Once our attention wanders, however, that's it. We're on autopilot. And as you know if you're a major worrier, it's on autopilot where so many of your worries appear. You don't remember walking to the corner shop because you've been going through what you'll say to your boss.

Psychologist and neuroscientist, Professor Ian Robertson, developed the Sustained Attention Response (SART) test, now used all over the world to assess a range of conditions from depression to Alzheimer's disease. Challenge, Professor Robertson outlines,[1] gets us out of absentmindedness and noticing something new helps us pay attention.

The key chemical messenger that helps us pay attention is noradrenaline. The part of the brain releasing the noradrenaline is also responsible for self-awareness. Professor Robertson refers to a major study[2] of over 2,000 people that showed we are no happier daydreaming than we are cleaning. It seems we're wired up to dwell and worry. The reason you scrutinize yourself when you're anxious is because, as Professor Robertson explains, the brain is like a magnifying glass on your negative thoughts. 'When we are anxious our mind becomes like a missile defence system on the watch for incoming threats […] with the sensitivity of the system turned up high enough, it will always find a potential threat, however, tiny.'[3]

On a scale of 1–10 how focused are you on tasks?
What one single action could give you more focus?

PROFESSOR ROBERTSON ON CUTTING DOWN SOCIAL MEDIA

'It's advisable to use social media sparingly. The evidence is that the more often social media is used, the lower the mood. This is especially true for younger people whose personality is still developing and who are trying to find their place in the world.

Limit your number of friends on Facebook, and certainly limit the times you look at it and the time you spend on it. Constantly looking at social media corrodes attention. The wandering mind is an unhappy mind, so the biggest protector is our capacity to focus attention. Social media doesn't train us to focus attention. Once the mind starts wandering, it's more likely to be negative. Switching attention between different forms of social media, like going from Facebook to Twitter and back, further corrodes your ability for sustained attention and that means you are corroding your greatest protector for controlling your own mood.'

6. BELIEVING YOU HAVE A FIXED PERSONALITY

This is a point we made in our first book, *Real Confidence*, and our third, *Real Ambition*, based on the work of professor of psychology at Stanford University Carol Dweck[4] who developed the theory of mindset. Some people have a fixed mindset and believe they are the way they are and can't change. Others have what Dweck terms a growth mindset. These people believe it's possible to change, whether that means learning a new skill, unlearning a bad habit, changing their lifestyle or changing their attitudes. To go from stressed to calm will inevitably require changes on your part, and these changes might challenge some of your self-beliefs.

As a clinical psychologist before he became a neuroscientist, Professor Robertson found that patients who felt their problems were beyond their control took the longest to help. Both Professor Robertson's experience and research underline that people who experience prolonged stress or severe anxiety have beliefs, attitudes and habitual thinking patterns that tend to perpetuate the stress. This may sound harsh out of context, but viewed from a neuroscience point of view – how your brain is functioning – the fixed views don't help your brain fire up what it needs to stop you from feeling anxious. A sense that you *can* change is enough to reduce the amount of cortisol flooding your brain and causing anxious thoughts. But the change has to happen in your actions. You can't tell yourself you believe you're capable of calming down. It's the actions that change your feelings.

As you are reading this book, you might hear yourself think certain statements: that's definitely not me, I could never do that, no way is that right for me. It's good to make a note of these thoughts and then really consider where these statements come from. If you had a fixed mindset you wouldn't believe real calm is possible, which is why we're confident you can find ways to avoid this obstacle.

Complete the following: I am not a _____
person

What one action can you take to prove yourself even just a little wrong?

PROFESSOR ROBERTSON ON THE BIGGEST MENTAL TRAPS

'A fatalistic approach is the biggest trap of all. The biggest saboteur is the belief that people don't have control over their emotions.

Sometimes the sources of fatalism can be genetic: "My mother was like this", "I've inherited this", or "I had terrible early or later experiences so I can't help the way I am now", or "I have this terrible job and there's nothing I can do about it". There is always something you can do in every situation, there is something you can change about yourself and how you respond.

There is no early experience you can't to some extent learn to adapt. You might never have had a proper secure attachment to your mother, which for sure will make you more vulnerable to anxiety. But we can control the brain. It can be easier or harder depending on one's background, it can take a long time, there may be many trials, but for sure all of us can control our emotions.

Sometimes what we need to be calm is to learn to be more assertive.

Handicapping beliefs, like perfectionism, are a great torture and source of anxiety. If you set out to make the best cake, you won't be calm. You are dooming yourself to failure. There will always be a better cake somewhere.

You're doomed if you combine a handicapped belief with an inauthentic ambition like "I want to win the Great British Bake Off". Statistically this is highly unlikely. But wanting to be a great baker is an authentic ambition and it's achievable.

You have to be good at setting goals for yourself. Not being good at setting goals can be due to false standards like a perfect body, celebrity, being top of class. These idealized images of what your standards should be lead to a constant state of anxiety because you are constantly failing against impossible ideas.'

We've presented just six stress triggers and outlined how you can avoid these. There might be one dominant trigger that jumps out, yet it's most likely to be a combination of all six. Ignoring your nature and what you truly need puts you in situations of adding pressure to your life. Developing self-compassion will help you avoid the damaging effect critical people can have on you. Self-compassion can include self-awareness, so check your ego and consider whether you're holding onto stressful situations because these are an ego booster.

One of the most crucial obstacles is a wandering mind because wandering minds tend to worry, so anything – any activity – that helps you focus your mind will be a huge booster. Unfortunately, one of the biggest elements of modern life, social media, encourages the mind to wander, so getting a handle on this is vital. Learning to avoid all these obstacles is possible with an open growth mindset. If you're fixed you will be rigid about what you can and can't do, your goals will limit you by trapping you in impossible scenarios.

"I faced up to having to learn about technology" *– Marion*

'I've been anxious ever since I can remember as a child and therapy has certainly helped me understand why. But understanding isn't enough. I still hid behind my anxiety. When it dawned on me that I just didn't know how to handle certain technology, rather than being technophobic, a light bulb flashed. I didn't need to run myself down for lack of skills that I could go out and learn.

I hadn't worked in an office for nearly two decades so I'd never been eased into new technology or had training. I would get into a major panic and my whole day would be ruined if I couldn't handle something. Until I could get hold of someone who could help, I'd be a wreck. If I couldn't access my emails my heart would be pounding. I'd lose something on the computer and I'd be shaking.

I realized I made a joke about being hopeless with technology, but a bigger realization was that it wasn't a joke, it was a negative mindset. This mindset was running my life and ruining my self-esteem because I held it up as evidence of being hopeless, and was then ashamed of myself.

I hadn't thought of the most obvious until a new web designer client asked me if I was really technophobic or simply didn't have the knowledge. She pointed out that there were courses available – and that people in IT were trained to do what they do, i.e. they learnt these skills.

Her advice was that the next time someone helped me, I should ask to learn from them instead of going into frazzled victim mode.

The first time I tried that was with my nephew fixing something on Facebook. It was so simple, I thought well even I could do that. This gave me some confidence so I booked to do various courses at a great adult education centre. I was surprised to meet people of all ages from 20–80. I'd wasted all that energy feeling ashamed that I was incapable of handling this monster technology. I faced up to having to learn about technology.

I also lined up a proper support system: I contacted all the local IT experts whose leaflets I'd collected to work out who I would trust and feel comfortable with in an emergency. My web design client designed my new website, showed me how to handle the basics, and looked after anything else. I felt so stupid realizing that I'd panicked over things that were an expert's job – again, what a waste of energy. Every time I meet a technology geek now I ask them a question. Often they say they don't know!

This hasn't happened overnight, and it's an ongoing process, but I've learnt that's normal because technology changes. Knowing the wi-fi is down because of an area problem and not some mystical monster means I don't panic and go to pieces because I can't get on with work. I go to the library. I don't get hysterical when there's a technology glitch. I keep calm because I know it's just machines, bits of metal that can be replaced if need be and certainly not "proof" that I am hopeless and incompetent.'

ASK YOURSELF

Is there an area in your life where you're operating against what feels natural to you? (E.g. forcing yourself to be party person, dressing to please a partner, putting on a front at work.)

What are your main personality traits? How do these fit with stress?

How focused are you? Do you find it hard to concentrate or complete tasks?

How much time do you spend on social media? What are the different emotions you experience through social media – negative and positive?

Are there any fixed statements you hear yourself make about yourself? (E.g. I'm rubbish at exercise, I'm hopeless at meditating, I'm technophobic.) Can you challenge these? How can you reframe these statements? (E.g. I haven't yet found a form of exercise I enjoy, but I'm looking; I haven't found a meditation teacher I've clicked with, but I'll give it another go; I don't know enough about technology, but I can learn.)

3 HOW CAN YOU BE CALM?

CHAPTER 7

CAN YOU LEARN TO BE CALM?

One of the many downsides to stress is the creeping belief settling in your mind that maybe you can't ever be calm. We hope that by this stage you'll feel more confident in your analysis of why you find yourself stressed and that this gives you the a-ha moments of recognizing what's going on in your brain and how this affects you. These a-ha moments are your launch pad for learning to be calm. We hope that the research and the advice from our experts has already reassured you that yes, it's possible to change.

In Part One we focused on what it really means to be calm, steering you towards a new definition based on being your best you as well as developing the skill of calm for when it's necessary. Then in Part Two we examined the reasons you might not be able to deal with stress, from how you were brought up to handle pressure, to understanding what you are experiencing right now. We presented six stress triggers which sabotage all your efforts to be calm.

You may find that by making some adaptations to how you handle stress, you don't need to learn to be calm for the most part. Yet modern life being the way it is, learning to be calm is an essential skill. In this final Part Three we will outline what it is you need to learn to be calm.

> *Stop: Telling yourself (or letting anyone else) tell you that you're hopeless at slowing down*
>
> *Start: Telling yourself (and everyone else) that you're learning to handle stress*

UNDERSTANDING THE BRAIN

We've aimed to demystify the brain for you, so that you realize you can tweak it. The more you learn about the brain and how it works, the more you know what the brain needs to boost your mind.

The brain is so plastic that it can adapt even during periods of acute stress. Research at the Rockefeller University[1] found that although chronic stress affects the brain's neural circuitry, keeping it 'trapped' in states of anxiety and depression, recovery *is* possible. Glutamate, the chemical signal affected during stress, has 'windows' of neuroplasticity.

Neuroscience expert Professor Ian Robertson believes that the key is learning how to *respond* to stress. Learning to view stress as a healthy challenge can help enormously. We don't need to allow our ancient brain to launch into fight or flight. It's about learning to take advantage of the brain's ability to change through experience. It's about mind management.

Professor Robertson's book outlines the ample research that the human brain *can* change through experience. Experience is the crucial point. You might think there's a chicken and egg situation here: how can you change your experience from frazzled to calm when you're too frazzled to think straight?

Understanding what happens in the brain can inspire you to make some simple changes. Professor Robertson refers to research[2] that demonstrated the way genes in the brain can change. The proteins 'expressed' by the brain's genes control functions in our bodies, including behaviour. Experiences and environment can turn *off* the genes' protein synthesizing activity, and this is especially the case with stress. Let's say this in simple words: Stress switches off your brain's ability to change.

When you're stressed you're often on autopilot, trying to survive and get by, and the last thing you might feel like doing is making an effort to go to a new restaurant, or try a new activity, so there's another vicious cycle. But the smallest changes can get you in the mood for change – and make a difference to your mood. From choosing a different coffee to taking a different route home, from eating a different cuisine to booking a different type of holiday, when you begin to introduce changes you are boosting your brain's ability to change. As we saw in the last chapter, a wandering mind isn't conducive to calmness, so when you make changes you're also helping yourself to be alert.

Stop: Following identical routines every day

Start: Making small changes to your choices

YOU CAN'T HURRY CALM

We saw in the previous chapter that making calm the goal triggers more stress, so how does that tie in with learning to be calm? Well this is all about you – that calm Holiday-You, your best you. The more you learn about yourself, identify what you need and learn to cultivate bringing this into your life, the calmer you will feel. Cynics of course will retort that this is nonsense. Of course you know yourself. And yes, you do, but when modern life takes over and you're living an overwhelmed life, eventually that little you is buried under responsibilities trying to cope. Stress becomes a wall around you and you can't recognize yourself. The reality is that the further along the continuum you are, the more time you need to recover your true self.

This isn't an instant process. It's a slow, organic one. We've been giving you a range of tips to help make that calm feeling you yearn for accessible, from taking a six-day holiday to bringing some Danish candle-lit 'hygge' into your life. But these tips in isolation are not enough. They are another layer.

All of this might seem frustrating if you want to calm down right now. Wanting an instant fix when you're stressed is natural. Understanding why you want a quick fix in relation to what's happening in the mind can help you deal with what mindfulness expert Ed Halliwell calls a 'mismatch' of modes. When the fight or flight system kicks off in your brain, you're wired up to *do* something. But the doing mode is not equipped to solve feelings of worry, stress, anxiety, depression.

First you need to slow down and be with yourself, taking time to appreciate what you need. When you learn to be with yourself, calm follows.

> **"People want a quick fix because of the human survival instinct. There is a threat alert which feels unpleasant and uncomfortable and we want to get out fast."**
>
> Ed Halliwell, mindfulness teacher and writer

Stop: Looking for a quick fix when you're wound up

Start: Looking to accumulate calm fixes throughout your day

SANDRA ELSDON VIGON ON TAKING TIME TO HEAL

'I always tell people when they come to me that the process of healing is not easy or quick. It's a big commitment to yourself that requires taking yourself and the process seriously.

A lot of what I do is helping people to slow down. Our culture is more hyped up than ever. It's Hurry Up and Be Calm. People are conditioned to want a quick fix.

But we need to wake up and listen to our bodies, our gut and our intuition. We need to ask: What do I need to change in my life?

It's not enough to identify emotions. We need to go deeper. How does it feel to feel anger, resentment, bitterness, for example? This takes us further into the process and makes healing possible.'

LEARN TO IDENTIFY YOUR STRESSED HABITS

You can't go from stressed to calm without a conscious awareness of how you behave and appear during any form of stress. Does your voice become shrill? Do you get snappy? Do you put on a glazed smile? All too often people want to reach a state of calm without a conscious awareness of their stressed state. It's like wanting to swim to the opposite side of the channel while drowning. Pretty impossible.

In Chapter 3 we gave you an idea of how real calm feels, and this included the fact that others experience you as calm. When people don't see you as nervous or anxious you are able to shine. Identifying your nervous habits, however, can take some investigation. You spend most of your waking hours working, and during those hours you have probably found a way to disguise the stress surging inside you. This might be so natural to you that you are unaware of all your efforts to do so. Learning to uncover where and how you dump and disguise your stress, from tensing up in your body to raising your voice, is a crucial learning process. Only then can you begin to find alternative ways to release the stress.

Stop: Being unkind to yourself about looking stressed

Start: Noticing where and how you feel tense in your body

" Your habits got you to where you are, so they have been useful. But are they useful all the time? What shifts do you need to make right now? "

Charlie Walker-Wise, RADA in Business trainer

CHARLIE WALKER-WISE ON THE EFFECT OF DISGUISING STRESS

'Being approachable is about how you show up. Are you able to be relaxed and confident? Or do you feel so vulnerable you are covering this up – which makes you less approachable? If what's going on inside is fear and stress, and you don't want others to know this, that energy often leaks, and the result at its most extreme will be that people don't want to deal with you.

When you are worried, nervous or stressed because of a business meeting or presentation and you're trying to cover this up, then this negative inner energy leaks out into the body: foot tapping, eyes blinking, playing with your hair, pulling your shirt down, fiddling with your pockets, twiddling your rings. This leakage of nervous energy lets people know you are not relaxed. They may not internalize that you are stressed, but their focus can be distracted by the evidence of this tension and the business message you are trying to communicate to them gets lost.

Leaders need to communicate to their teams – and be available to people. Are you someone who people can approach? Do you make yourself approachable? When you are communicating, do you present yourself in a way that says: "I am open to ideas?"'

IT'S ALL ABOUT TRAINING

Learning implies that there are facts, concepts and processes to learn and remember. But the word training is probably far more accurate in the context of calmness. You don't need to learn anything because you don't need to consciously remember to do anything. When you train your mind to handle stress, your mind develops the ability to focus on looking after you. When you train, you become conscious of what it is you need to do to look after yourself.

What you train in is up to you. We will give you recommendations, but the key is to find a form of training that works for you. Anything from setting out to make a daily lifestyle change, to going on a mindfulness course to learn specific mental techniques, can help you. We don't believe in prescribing any one way, but we do know that you have to find what works for you.

This could be a practical skill like tackling an issue you're not confident in. To become competent inevitably you have to work at 'it' whatever 'it' is. RADA in Business trainer Charlie Walker-Wise says it's not uncommon for people to have a hang-up about their voices which makes them nervous about presenting. 'We give people a voice exercise regime and suggest they practise three times a week for a few minutes for six weeks. You can learn all sorts of skills but if you want to change you have to practise.'

Rather than a practical skill, you may find what you need is to learn specific relaxation techniques. Again, these need practice so that they become regular conscious habits.

> ❝There are many relaxation techniques. But they are just that: techniques. You can do something else like go for a walk.❞
>
> Jeremy Stockwell, performance consultant and TV coach

Stop: Saying you've no time to learn anything
Start: Exploring what would be fun to learn

'If you think about training to run a marathon, who expects to prepare to run a marathon in 20 minutes? It takes work and time, and you have to cultivate your body and your attitude. You don't throw yourself into a marathon as you would injure yourself. The same is true of working with the mind, if not more so.

We need to go gently. Patterns might be entrenched, but we can train to change these. Over time we can drop into greater self-compassion, patience and connection to the world. But we can't snap into it.

Any skill requires practice – it's the 10,000 hour rule. You can't suddenly be a concert pianist. The mind is like an instrument. If you want to be with the mind like a musician with an instrument, then you have to practise.

The working definition I use for mindfulness is a slight adaptation from Jon Kabat-Zinn's (Professor of Medicine Emeritus and creator of the Stress Reduction Clinic and the Center for Mindfulness in Medicine, Health Care, and Society at the University of Massachusetts Medical School): An awareness and approach to life that arises from paying attention, on purpose, fully present with curiosity and kindness.

We need to train our attention to attend to our life in a skillful way, moving away from partial attention and training ourselves to put our minds on where we want to go, rather than always following distraction. We need to recognize when our mind is wandering. It's like training the body in the gym again and again.

Mindfulness is a sensory experience. The word mindfulness is not actually that helpful as it can imply this is about being in the head. Our experiences like anxiety are in the body as much as the mind.

We need to be curious about what's going on in our experience and we need to give ourselves kindness, the antidote to the self-critical "why can't I make myself better approach" which doesn't make us better.

Mindfulness is knowing what's happening as its happening and learning from this. It's:

A. *awareness*
B. *being with our experience*
C. *choice.*

If we know what's happening and let go of our automatic reactions, then we start to develop freedom of choice. We can learn how to work with mind and body so we can live in a more skillful way.'

The crux of this chapter is that the more you learn about yourself, the more you can learn to be calm. Learning to be calm is a process that develops naturally, albeit slowly, as soon as you begin to heal whatever needs to be healed and as soon as you identify what you need.

Of course there are practical skills that you might believe are essential, like making effective business presentations and being able to talk to your team without getting agitated. These aren't as rigidly based on learning rules as you might imagine. Communicating effectively is about learning to get rid of tension in the body and the mind and the starting point is learning where and how you store tension and nervous habits. We hope you'll be fascinated to learn how words come out of our mouth and be poised to learn more about calm communication.

One of our themes in this book is a mindful understanding of oneself, by which we mean a kind appraisal of who you are. The biggest challenge is learning to be kind to yourself.

REAL PEOPLE

"I tried everything from CBT to NLP to conquer anxiety" – *Anita*

'I've been anxious ever since I can remember, and with age and hormones it got worse. To a certain extent I could hide behind the demands of my career, but I knew my anxiety had deeper roots. I've tried most talking therapies since I started therapy at 20.

My first therapist at university gave me the best advice: you have to make the decision to change your life and take positive actions. I realized that understanding why you are the way you are isn't about blaming anyone or circumstances. It's about knowing yourself and being kind to yourself.

My childhood was difficult for good reason: my parents were immigrants, they were forced out of their country, they were worried about relatives, they had financial problems, they struggled with the language and we experienced racism. I understood through therapy that my father was authoritarian in order to cope and survive, my mother was controlling about cleanliness and meal times because that was all she could control. Then there were all the cultural and religious rules they carried.

I was diagnosed in my 20s with generalised anxiety disorder. All the talking therapies and everything else I looked into, from rebirthing to past lives, not only helped me cope but also gave me hope, never mind that some of these were bonkers and possibly bogus.

I was and am determined to feel better. I have accepted that maybe I'll always be a little anxious – but at least I'm not bitter, angry, lonely, unfulfilled. I learnt to use my anxiety, turning it into the voice of reason. My clients value me because I think before I risk their money. My "risky" male colleagues quietly turn to me for an opinion when they're having second thoughts.

Everyone is different and I think it's dangerous to insist there is any one miracle way. A big factor is the therapist rather than the label of what they are practising. For the past eight years I have seen a counsellor every week for a couple of months of the year when I feel everything getting on top of me. I have made the biggest leaps and positive changes with her. This is someone who reminds me that there are legitimate reasons to be anxious and I don't need to feel guilty about fear of redundancy and the future when it's a real possibility. But I can take action to prepare. Here is someone who reminds me that going to yoga and Tai Chi makes me feel relaxed and helps me sleep. She listens, and she smiles. She reminds me of how far I've come.

One "friend" suggested I was dependent on my counsellor – and I replied as gently as I could that I prefer this way to drinking a bottle of wine every night. We all have our ways of coping. I am aware as a parent that I am over cautious, but thankfully my partner is the opposite to me. He is the one encouraging our two children to do all sorts of activities, I am the one shrieking "OMG you'll fall off, you'll drown, you'll break your leg". He makes a siren noise which makes the kids laugh (and eventually me too). More than seeing them grow up fearless, I want them to grow up minus a terrified voice in their heads.'

ASK YOURSELF

Q What's a simple and specific change that you can make to your daily life to improve the quality of your life?

Q What do you instinctively know you need time to heal?

Q What are your stressed habits? What do you do when you are anxious?

Q What could you learn that would help you right now?

CHAPTER 8

LIVING YOUR OWN VERSION OF CALM

I f you've been living for some time in a stressed anxious state, or if you can always remember worrying about things since you were a child, it's likely that you have absorbed a certain belief that your worry, anxiety and stress are normal and even necessary. When worry becomes a habit, and living under stress is the norm, people fall into the trap of believing that there's no other option. If you didn't worry about your family's dramas you'd be selfish, if you didn't take on your workload the company you work for would suffer, if you said no to social commitments you'd hurt and upset people. These are all misbeliefs.

Part of learning to be calm involves learning to reframe these entrenched beliefs that have been creating fear in your life. A major part of real calm is being yourself, and you cannot be yourself if you are beholden to others. You won't be cold and clinical when you are calm, and neither will you be so laid back that you're irresponsible and inefficient. Learning to lead a calm life also benefits others around you. Real calm is about looking after ourselves as individuals so that we can also look after others and be valuable to the world.

So let's clarify what that means.

YOU DESCRIBE LIFE AS BALANCED

When you think of the epitome of a calm person, it's very likely that the image that will come into your head is that of a Buddhist monk. But this isn't helpful on an everyday basis is it? You're entirely right: it's not practical, viable or even desirable.

It's a Buddhist monk's job to be calm. In any religious order, monks and nuns devote their lives to contemplation, living away from modern life and leading a very simple existence. That's their choice, not yours. It's more than likely that your choice is to create the best life you can for yourself in the midst of modern life.

If your job is in any way demanding, competitive, exciting, pressurized, your priority will be to learn how to thrive under stress. To do this you'll be looking to balance the demands of work with activities outside work that benefit your body and mind. And the key is the word balance. If one area of your life is more pressurized, another needs to be more restorative.

> " We need to strive for a pragmatic balance in our lives, between go-go-go on one side and relaxing, re-energizing and renewing ourselves on the other. This means looking at our time and making decisions about it. "
>
> Miriam Akhtar, positive psychologist

Balance, however, doesn't just come from calculating what we do in different areas of our life. Balance also comes from cultivating a certain mental and meaningful approach to life. We might not be Tibetan monks, but a degree of contemplation about the meaning of our lives can enrich them and provide balance. Life doesn't have to be a treadmill. What's it all for, what's it all about, what's the point, what gives you satisfaction, what makes you happy, what gives you joy, who can you give joy to – these are far from self-indulgent questions, they are essential for a calm life.

SANDRA ELSDON VIGON ON FINDING
MEANING IN LIFE

'When you know who you are and you trust your instincts,
your intuition, your gut feeling and you live your life from that
place, that's living a soulful, meaningful life.

We need meaning in life because life is difficult and we need
to feed our souls. There are many ways in which we can do
this. For some people this might be spiritual, for others it can
be something creative. Creativity is not just an activity but
also an attitude.

A meaningful life has joy. It's so wonderful to watch children
and dogs because they are in the moment. They don't care
or think about anything else but that moment, and for us
adults in this crazy world we have to find a version of this for
ourselves.'

YOU CHOOSE WHEN YOU WANT TO BE CALM

Yes, calm is a choice. If there's only one thing we hope you take
away from this book it's that you can learn to feel calm *when* you
want to be so – which isn't always.

> " **Calmness is a positive attribute
> but not at the cost of our
> vitality. If you're calm in a
> floppy, disengaged way where
> is your vitality?** "

Charlie Walker-Wise, RADA in Business trainer

When you lead a calm life, essentially you know how to avoid dramas – internally and externally. Life is calm because there is an absence of unnecessary conflict, enabling you to handle the unavoidable problems that come up with disputes. If you're embroiled in dysfunctional friendships and relationships which are stressful, or if you voluntarily take on far more than you can handle, then the reality is you'll feel too drained to deal with a demanding job. Strip away what drains you and that job might be rewarding, satisfying and even exciting.

All of this is about fine tuning the various elements of your life and how your mind responds. Only you know this.

DECOMPRESS

American anxiety specialist Reneau Z. Peurifoy recommends creating decompression routines.[1] Developing rituals or routines to allow the mind and body to recover between activities or areas of life allows them to recover. Instead of going from one activity to the other, rushing to juggle different roles in your life, stop briefly to decompress.

Taking just a few minutes can provide the mental punctuation you need to stop you getting overwhelmed and suffering from stress. 'Accept your body is a machine with a limited supply of energy,' writes Peurifoy,[2] advising regular rest, scheduled relaxation, maintenance and care, as well as humour and support.

Make sure the decompression routine does not involve your smartphone or computer and that you are fully immersed in it –

whether it's singing along to your favourite song or watching the birds outside the window or savouring a cup of green tea.

YOU EMBRACE STRESS

Within limits you can harness stress into a positive energy because the same symptoms as excitement underlie stress. Just describing your anxiety as excitement will make you feel better. As Professor Robertson points out in his book,[3] we don't always read our emotions accurately. Many emotional states share similar symptoms: anxiety, sexual arousal, anger – and excitement – have similar symptoms. By recognizing and renaming your emotions you are their master rather than being controlled by them.

> "We want to be calm because stress is unpleasant. But stress is also necessary for us to perform."
>
> Professor Ian Robertson, psychologist and neuroscientist

A study by Alison Brooks at the University of Pennsylvania, published by the American Psychological Association,[4] confirmed that people who get excited and think about what can go well instead of focusing on what can go wrong perform better in situations provoking anxiety. The study reported on a number of experiments at Harvard University with students and local community members. The participants in one experiment who were told to repeat 'I am excited' before delivering a speech were rated by independent evaluators as more competent, persuasive and relaxed than those who had to repeat 'I am calm'. In another experiment involving a difficult mathematics test, the group instructed to 'try to get excited' performed best. In a karaoke trial, 113 participants were randomly told to say they were anxious, excited, calm, angry or sad before singing karaoke on a rated system. Everybody's heart rate was monitored to measure anxiety. The excited group were rated 80% by the video game system, while the calm, angry, sad groups scored an average 69%, and the anxious group scored 53%. The excited group also felt excited and confident.

By rebranding what you're experiencing from stress to excitement, the science shows that not only can you deal with stress effectively, you will also perform better. Rather than experiencing calmness, you are not experiencing horrible stress.

> "The symptoms of stress are similar to excitement: a fast pulse, a dry mouth, a churning tummy. If you can tell yourself you are excited about taking on a challenge, the chemistry in your brain changes because you are not under threat."
>
> Professor Ian Robertson, psychologist and neuroscientist

PROFESSOR ROBERTSON ON HOW TO ADJUST YOUR SWEET SPOT FOR STRESS

'If you are watching a film eating popcorn and you are too sluggish you will fall asleep, so you need a level of noradrenaline activation to keep the brain alert. But this level will be much lower than chairing a meeting with colleagues, where you will need higher levels of noradrenaline. In terms of calmness you don't want to be laid back because if your *arousal is too low, your response won't be fast – and in a business situation you need to be fast.*

If you are having dinner with your partner, and you are still in a hyped-up state after a day's work, still checking messages on your smartphone, then you need to pull your sweet spot down, so your level of arousal is down.

It's a constant search for the appropriate level, knowing when you're tipped beyond your spot, what it is that tips you.'

YOU'RE A GREAT COMMUNICATOR

Dealing with other people is one of the biggest reasons people feel they need to calm down. Whether anxiety makes you withdraw from the world, or stress has you barking at anyone who tips you beyond your limits, you're suffering as a result of not being able to communicate. You feel resentful because you're not heard, or guilty because you unleashed your voice in order to be heard.

Calm communication doesn't mean you'll be clinical. On the contrary you will be more engaged and effective. Neither does calm communication mean you have to learn to master anything that (for the moment) seems stressful, like public speaking. As we've outlined in our definition of real calm, it's about being you and the biggest part of you is how you communicate. Both RADA in Business trainer Charlie Walker-Wise and RADA/BBC coach Jeremy Stockwell do not train their business clients to deliver presentations in a set way.

'I try not to give my clients generic advice,' says Stockwell, himself a performer and theatre maker. His emphasis is on training all clients, whether they are actors or come from the business and political world, to be themselves in the moment, focusing on a calm and natural connection with their audience.

CHARLIE WALKER-WISE ON THE SKILL OF CALM COMMUNICATION

'If you cannot communicate your [business] ideas and share these in a way that connects them to people, then you don't reach people.

To reach people you need to start with a calm awareness of yourself and to develop an awareness of others.

One of the exercises I use at RADA in Business is called Open Window–Closed Window to illustrate the different modes we operate in.

At work people operate mostly in Closed-Window mode. I ask people attending training workshops to lower their eye level and put their hands by their eyes like horse blinkers. The response is immediate: it doesn't feel good, it feels like others around might be a threat. Yet this is how people are sitting at their desks for hours at work.

In the Open-Window mode I ask people to open their arms out like aeroplane wings, and be aware of their fingers at eye level in their peripheral vision. Immediately they feel more alert, energized, positive, and they feel good about sharing space with others.

I ask people to move around in the room and notice their feelings when they work with these two different ways of being.

Even outside work people stay in Closed-Window mode, walking down the street looking at their phones, not being present, or looking down worrying.

In Open-Window mode we have peripheral vision and an awareness of space. We are present, conscious of our surroundings.

When you open yourself up, then you engage with what is in front of you, which makes you feel better – not worried, anxious, stressed.

There are times when we can't be available and need to be in Closed-Window mode to concentrate and focus, whether it's to write a report or respond to important emails.

But when we want to engage with people – and much of business is about engaging with people – then we need to come out of that into Open-Window mode. As soon as we expand our bodies we feel better.'

Life when you're calm doesn't mean you'll morph into a Buddhist monk or that you'll be floating around in the clouds. You will be living and experiencing your life as balanced, and feel that your life is meaningful. Stress won't frighten you; on the contrary, you'll have the energy to take on exciting challenges, the ability to recognize when you need to pull back, and the skill to master rebranding stress that you do feel into excitement. You'll be communicating effectively and confidently, not only avoiding conflict, but confidently getting across your message.

REAL PEOPLE

"I used to be detached – now I really can be calm" *– Tim*

'I'm known at work as Mr Nice Guy. Colleagues and clients have always said I'm calm. When I realized I had this constant low level of anxiety, I started to panic. I worried that I was a fraud and sooner or later I'd crack, explode, not hold it together and that would be it.

I soldiered on, playing computer games to relax after work, eating and drinking more than government health recommendations. My ex-partner worked long hours too, and we'd get ready meals or takeaways. Every year we'd join a gym and I'd go once. Every year she did a January detox. Deep down I knew the relationship was stagnant. But it was comfortable. Then we split. She wanted to get married and have children before it was too late for her, and although I didn't say no, she got angry that I wasn't into the idea. I wasn't exactly demonstrating excitement.

Part of me was relieved we split up, part of me felt guilty, but I was utterly heart-broken, lonely, and every day I worried about absolutely everything from my ageing parents to the firm losing business.

I started going to a local sports centre because I saw a notice that they had Tai Chi classes. I'd always fancied the idea of Tai Chi because people looked so calm in photos. Being at a local sports centre rather than a snobby gym meant there were all sorts of normal people, not just shiny hipsters working out their perfect bodies. The trainer who gave me my induction course said a lot of the members went to relieve stress and for fun. His advice was to try every class on the programme * just for fun*. So I even tried Zumba. I'm pretty introverted and shy, and I was the only bloke hiding at the back. Yes, it was fun.

I've been going religiously to Tai Chi and yoga because I feel so good afterwards. The effects were immediate from the first classes; even though I had no coordination or flexibility, I realized it's not about that. I go to kick boxing which is great for letting off steam, and circuit classes which get all my nervous energy out. Instead of just being a commuter, I feel part of a community now because so many people say hi to me in the neighbourhood. Knowing I have a class to get to means I leave work on time. Saying to partners in the firm or even clients that I've got to get to Tai Chi or kick boxing was easier than I thought it would be. I used to be Mr Always Available. Now no one takes me for granted.

I've been on adventure holidays, like rock climbing and deep sea diving, and once a year I go to a retreat for yoga, meditation or Tai Chi. I still love my food, I still enjoy my wine. But my body wants to eat well and, check me out, I'm even cooking. It's how I relax.

I really am calm now – before I was detached and a bit dead. I feel alive now.'

ASK YOURSELF

In what way would you like your life to be calm?

What does the concept of meaning in life mean to you? What gives you meaning in your life?

Does being stressed make you unapproachable in any way?

In what way would you like your life to thrive on excitement and challenge?

CHAPTER 9

CALM BOOSTERS

Y ou have processed what happens in the brain when you're stressed and how your mind reacts to stress. Through our tests and Ask Yourself questions you've been able to analyse what real calm means to you. In Chapter 6 we gave you six stress triggers to be aware of and avoid. We're now ready with this chapter and the final one to give you specific guidelines.

The first dimension to real calm is self-awareness combined with self-compassion. With this understanding you can initiate calmness into your daily life so that it becomes your foundation. Like anything, you have to put your mind to it and invest in looking after yourself.

We've narrowed down six things that can boost your calmness. Just one of these alone might make a dramatic difference to your life, and as you read through you will sense what resonates most with you.

> **"We are like flowers in a garden, growing in different seasons, pollinated at different stages, flowering at different moments. So allow yourself time. Start now. Breathe."**
>
> Jeremy Stockwell, performance consultant and TV coach

1. RELATING TO OTHER PEOPLE

Human beings are social beings. The more stress you experience, the more likely it is that you feel isolated even if you're surrounded by people all the time. There's a misconception that connecting with people means baring and sharing all your woes. With some you will – with others you won't. Relating to others takes you out of the autopilot stressed mode that keeps you in your head. It tricks your brain into feeling way better.

Friends can be a major antidote to stress if you learn how to use friendships in a positive way. Rather than using friendships to moan or fill in time when you're bored, you can turn to friendships to provide a vital base for support and wellbeing. If you surround yourself only with stressed friends who perpetuate the cycle of stressed habits, you're not helping yourself. *New York Times* bestselling author and behaviour researcher Tom Rath[1] studied the Gallup Organization's research on friendship, as well as conducting experiments with a team of researchers. His findings illustrated that good friendships have a massive impact on individuals – from feeling more satisfied at work if you have a best friend there, to eating more healthily if your best friend is a healthy eater. Rath's philosophy on friendship is based on identifying the roles different friends play in our lives and not expecting one friend to be everything. Rath identifies eight vital roles friends can play: builder, champion, collaborator, companion, connector, energizer, mind opener and navigator. In terms of real calm, think about who in your friendship circle is a companion and energizer – who is always there for you, and who gives you a boost?

> " **Nourish a range of friendships at work and outside work. Don't expect one person to fulfil everything you need.** "
>
> Miriam Akhtar, positive psychologist

However difficult the environment you work in, rather than burying yourself behind a screen and your headphones, be open to finding supportive people so that you boost each other. This doesn't mean people who only gossip and moan as negative talk drags you down. Who can support you by giving you practical advice? Who can make you laugh and see the funny side? Who can you share a healthy lunch with? Who is up for a fun activity? Jane Dutton,[2] Professor of Business Administration and Psychology at Michigan Ross School of Business, has researched high-quality connections and relationships at work. Positive relationships in the workplace don't just help us survive, they help us thrive.

> ## All business comes down to good relationships. Can you cross the floor to speak to someone rather than emailing them?
>
> Miriam Akhtar, positive psychologist

Taking this principle one step further, you can start cultivating ways to gain support by joining a group that helps you train to deal with stress in a supportive environment, whether it's a yoga class or a mindfulness course. There's a huge sense of relief when you're in a room full of people who are there to destress, and a reminder that this is the human condition.

> ## Opening up and connecting to others helps us find skillful ways to be in life.
>
> Ed Halliwell, mindfulness teacher and writer

JEREMY STOCKWELL ON THE VALUE OF LEARNING TO RECEIVE

'The Japanese are culturally more receptive. When you meet somebody in New York the person takes off their hat and stands up. A Japanese person takes off their shoes and sits down. When you give your business card to an American, they put it in their pocket. A Japanese person takes it, holds it with care and inspects it. In Japan a measure of your generosity is how receptive you are. We can learn from this. When you go into a room, whether it's a business meeting or a social event, focus on receiving.

To truly give the best of yourself in any situation you need to be present in your body, mind and voice – and to be focusing on others. Where you might be nervous because perhaps you have a presentation or a business pitch, if you focus on others your nerves will disappear because you are not doing this for you.

We need to remember we are all interconnected. If you connect to your environment and the people in this environment, you will have a true sense of others and you will be able to proceed with equanimity.

When your focus is on pouring your stuff out at people, this pushes people away. When you're caught up in how nervous you are, the effect is to push people away too.

To receive authentically and appropriately we need to come away from judgement of ourselves and others. When you have to meet a group of people, breathe and receive them. Take a moment to breathe properly, with your entire lung capacity. Be aware of your feet – this grounds your body and opens your mind so that you're not caught up in nerves and *anxiety. In this condition, your meetings and interactions will be much more successful and the outcomes more fruitful.*

To be sensible means to be sense-able, to come into our senses. Receive through your senses: whatever your situation is, what can you see, hear, smell, touch, taste? When our five senses are working, then our sixth sense, intuition, is activated.

We are not broadcasters, we are receivers. Thinking is you talking to yourself, whereas sense is real, it's concrete. In this way, despite educational and media influences, you can learn to trust yourself a lot more. You will seem more responsible. Responsibility is the ability to respond: how will you respond in a given situation? When you focus on receiving your intuition, it will guide you and inspire you to respond. When you receive, you will be inspired.

That way everyone is calmer, others will trust you more and the outcomes – professional or personal – will be that much more successful.

2. MASTER CORRECT BREATHING

If there is just one skill that we absolutely recommend you learn, it's breathing. Our experts are unanimous on this. Even if you insist that meditation and mindfulness are too challenging for you (though we'd urge you to give everything a go) breathing is something we do constantly. So we may as well learn how to breathe properly. Breathing is the one process we can call on at any given time to change the chemistry in our mind. Understand breath and train to breathe, and you have an instant tranquillizer. In Chapter 3 we gave you our health guru and *Psychologies* columnist Andrew Weil's breathing technique and, if you've tried this out, hopefully you'll be nodding and smiling at this point.

CHARLIE WALKER-WISE ON UNDERSTANDING HOW WE BREATHE

'When we are stressed we have certain physiological responses which prevent us from breathing properly. But there is a lot of confusion about how to breathe. People tend to think of lungs being in the chest, but the bulk of the lungs are around the side of the ribcage and in our back. The impulse for the breath comes from the diaphragm, and when the diaphragm drops into the abdomen, it pulls the lungs down so that they increase in volume and air and squidge out of the way your intestines and stomach.

When you breathe like this, deep into the belly, you supply the body with the amount of oxygen it needs, particularly when you are doing something challenging, like a business presentation. You need to breathe this way when you most need to communicate, handle stress and deal with uncertain dynamics, in order to provide the brain with as much oxygen-rich blood as possible.

When people think about breathing they think about breathing IN, but when you are stressed you need to breathe OUT first – the breath in will follow without any effort.

Actors need to train to have a strong voice so they can resonate in a theatre, and they do this by building up strength to breathe out – because when you are speaking you breathe out, not in. To do that you need a musculature that's a bit like an accordion, which powers air out. In acting we talk about supported breath, using abdominal and intercostal muscles to power the breath; we talk about people being ON voice, using the mechanics of the body to fill a room with power and conviction.

> *There are similar situations in business. To engage these muscles you have to be calm, allowing a good amount of air before they can supply the voice with power. That's where that nervous energy comes in: you can put it THERE to create power, you can use all your nervous energy for a good cause.'*

3. DO MORE OF WHATEVER MAKES YOU FEEL GOOD

One of the world's leading authorities on positive emotions is award-winning Professor of Psychology at the University of Carolina, Barbara Fredrickson.[3] Through rigorous research she developed the broaden and build theory of positive emotions: broadening the range of positive emotions we experience helps us build resourcefulness that then enables us to deal with challenging situations in life. When you're going through a difficult time, however, this is mighty difficult. On holiday, away from it all, you can easily build on having a good time – you'll even try lots of new things. But in the midst of a crisis? Or when stress has worn you out so much life feels relentless, how does that work?

66 **Needing to escape from stressful times is understandable. But it is necessary to find something life affirming and make healthier choices other than getting drunk or high.** 99

Sandra Elsdon Vigon, Jungian psychotherapist

It's about finding moments of calmness through moments and times of escape and building on these. Doing more of what you love gives you pleasure. This means having hobbies that have nothing to do with achievement or making money, but are activities you enjoy. These activities clear your head, support you and nourish you. As Jungian psychotherapist Sandra Elsdon Vigon puts it, they help you enter a zone that 'provides a safe and protective space where there is no one to answer to'.

> **Fool around for no reason, without the need to prove something, with no desire for exact mastery, just for the joy of letting go, like dancing at a party for the joy of dancing.**
>
> Jeremy Stockwell, performance consultant and TV coach

RELEASE YOUR RAGE

Rage-ercise[4] is a combination of fitness and an outlet for rage and frustration. Trauma therapist Adele Theron originally came up with the idea to run Tantrum Club workshops[5] to help women release their emotions and get fit while also bonding together. However the concept is something that can be of benefit regardless of whether you're male or female. The principle behind these classes is

that suppressing emotions creates stress in the
body which has damaging effects on health. The
sessions involve healthier ways of letting off steam:
using baseball bats to pound pillows, stamping on
bubble wrap, writing angry thoughts on balloons and
popping them. Give it a go!

4. BE PREPARED

Life is about changes and challenges and there's no escaping
that, so all we can do is prepare to handle what comes up as best
as possible. Professor Robertson explains[6] that when the brain
reappraises negative events, this turns down the stress-linked activity
in the brain's main emotion centre, which helps us cope better in the
future. When the brain is under full emergency drill it's hard to do this.
'But if we practise we can get better. We can learn to accept the reality
of something that has happened without catastrophizing entirely.'

When we feel we're in control and can handle life, stress doesn't
get the better of us. When we feel wobbly it's like struggling to
walk on a conveyor belt – you can't keep up, your feet are out
of control. Anything you can actively do to prepare for difficult
situations coming up helps you develop a sense that you're not
out of control. Real calm is about developing competence so that
you can confidently face what needs to be faced, whether that's a
difficult person, a work challenge or a personal issue.

PROFESSOR ROBERTSON ON TRAINING TO DEAL WITH STRESS

*'You need to train yourself to handle situations that trigger
stress in the same way that the Special Forces train to
go into battlefields. Just as they have to create simulated
battle conditions, it's simply not enough to practise what*

makes us feel good. There's no point. We need to test the habits in situations where we need them. We can test in our minds, we can imagine, we can create mental states, we can imagine our boss shouting at us, or a text from an ex-partner. And then we can rehearse.

When you anticipate a difficult conversation, take a few moments beforehand to relax. You can visualise and hear in your mind what might happen and prepare for your response in advance. If you rehearse good responses, you are more likely to handle the situation well.'

5. TRAIN TO TAME THE MIND

There's ample scientific evidence that meditation benefits the brain. With so many different types of meditation, knowing where to start can be daunting. Mindfulness is the current buzzword, but you might also come across Zen, Buddhist and transcendental meditation.

There are broadly two types of meditation. One type is 'concentrative' or guided meditation where the focus is on specific thoughts and breathing, and the other is 'non directive' where the mind wanders. A team of researchers at the Norwegian University of Science and Technology (NTNU), the University of Oslo and the University of Sydney have been collaborating to find out exactly what happens in the brain during different types of meditation.[7] They have discovered that nondirective meditation leaves more room to process memories and emotions because the brain is able to rest from everything else it has to do.

Whatever you decide to try out or choose according to what's near you, is easily accessible and above all suits you, there's ample evidence for the benefits of any form of meditation. One study[8] even showed that meditation can boost unavoidable multitasking skills in information-intensive office environments because it improves concentration.

It's well worth trying out meditation because for the short amount of time in your day that you invest, the benefits are huge. A recent study[9] by Dawn Querstret and Professor Mark Cropley from Surrey University in partnership with the Mental Health Foundation found that just two hours of mindfulness training online over the course of a week can dramatically reduce fatigue and worry, leading to switching off and relaxing after work and sleeping better.

The challenge is to make any meditation practice a daily habit. As we pointed out in Chapter 7, learning to be calm is more about training and that requires patience. Don't worry if it feels difficult to start with because that's entirely normal.

ED HALLIWELL ON PRACTISING MINDFULNESS

'Mindfulness is like the playing the piano – it's difficult to teach yourself. It's not impossible, but it isn't easy and the best you can do is to train in easier circumstances. You can do that for five minutes at a time with an audio so you are guided through a meditation. (On my website there are guided meditations.) You train when you're not in a difficult situation, and then over time you bring that into difficult scenarios.

Ideally it's good to take a course too with a teacher you like. You wouldn't start your first swimming lesson in a stormy sea. You would do so in a contained space with support, a pool with a teacher. You're dealing with the mind which is complex and powerful. Often people give up because they try mindfulness during an acutely high-stress situation.

Most people come on courses because they are stressed. Stress signals to us something needs to happen and that something might be mindfulness. A one-day workshop is a good start to see how you get on and if you connect with the teacher.

Mindfulness is counter-intuitive, because we are invited to sit with the stress and deal with it. It's being rather than doing. Non-doing is not what we are trained to do. All of our evolutionary history says do something. This is why you need to find a good teacher. Everyone is unique and a teacher can see you properly and help you during a course.

Formal practice and skilled guidance gives you a context to work with during a difficult situation – but it doesn't guarantee immediate calm.

Mindfulness is about learning to be present, in the moment, rather than multitasking. There are other ways you can look to cultivating mindfulness. A yoga class can be a way of cultivating a connection between mind and body, for example. Some people find yoga more of a challenge than meditation.

My first mindfulness task was mindful tea drinking: to be fully aware of the sensation of the taste, touch, smell of a cup of tea and nothing else. There was an immediate calming effect from this. You can eat your lunch out of the storm of the office and really invite yourself to taste your food. When you're cleaning your teeth, you can totally experience this rather than getting habitually lost and not noticing your thoughts. This is a start on the path to mindfulness.'

6. A CALM BODY STEERING THE MIND

It's frustrating trying to change emotions that feel beyond your control. When you're in that spiral of worry, of course you'd snap out of it if you could, which is why being told to stop worrying makes you feel even more agitated.

When your mind feels like it's on a permanent spin dryer, it's all too easy to focus on the contents in that spin dryer as the route to calming down. You forget your body entirely because that's not the problem. And yet focusing on your body is the easiest route to handling the problem, namely your mind. This is the path actors routinely take so that we don't see them as gibbering wrecks and so that they *feel* able to handle nerves.

Taking the body route is something absolutely everybody can do. RADA in Business trainer Charlie Walker-Wise describes the process as one that moves people away from their heads. To explain why, he refers to his joy of being a parent, watching his child laughing as a baby and encouraging him to laugh and play. The normal cycle of childhood is to play and be encouraged, until, as Walker-Wise describes, children are told to 'act your age' and instead of playing they are encouraged to cram information into their heads.

The problem underlining the absence of calm is this crammed head we grow up to carry. It's not just information that we stuff our minds with, but thoughts that aren't useful. As you know all too well, when you're not calm you wish you could drill your head to let some of these thoughts escape. Instead of thinking your way out (or as is very common drinking to numb the thoughts), you can move your way through.

Several studies have shown that exercise improves the mood because of feel-good chemicals released in the brain. But more recent studies are showing that the benefits extend beyond an immediate positive change in mood. Exercise can help the brain deal with anxiety and stress.[10]

One recent study[11] by neuroscientists at the University of California showed why people who exercise have better mental fitness. Two important neurotransmitters, glutamate and gamma-aminobutyric acid or GABA, are released through intense exercise. Because vigorous exercise can be more demanding for the brain than something mentally challenging, the researchers explained that the brain makes more neurotransmitters. Studies like this are leading the way in establishing exercise as an alternative to anti-depressant medication.

> " We end up with no relationship with our body. It's twisted and tense and our mind is going: why am I so stressed? To be calm we need to use our physicality. "
>
> Charlie Walker-Wise, RADA in Business trainer

You might not like the sound of exercise, but that could be because you associate it with doomed January New Year resolutions to join a gym and lose weight. But so long as you consider that calm can come from using your body, how you do so is up to you. That could include turning your Strictly Come Dancing TV habit into ballroom dancing classes, or having regular shoulder massages to dispel the tension from sitting at a desk. You could let off steam with kick boxing or unwind with something mellow like Tai Chi. Even getting up from your desk regularly and stretching can make a huge difference to how your mind handles stress.

REMEMBER YOUR CALM BOOSTERS

We think you'll agree that our six recommended ways to a calm you are not complicated. Connecting with people might sound overwhelming if you've been through a hard time, but this isn't about dressing up and going to parties. You might make a concerted effort to see friends who are good listeners or join a new network with likeminded people. This can be the first step to feeling better and more able to tackle what's causing stress. As soon as you take away the focus from you and turn your attention to who you are with, you'll find you can escape from your stressed nervous head.

Learning to breathe is a valuable skill we recommend you master. It's the one skill you can call on at any time to change the chemistry in your mind. And since you are already breathing, it's a goal that's 100% attainable. So is doing more of what you love, whatever that is. Our *Real Ambition* book outlined that the work-til-you-drop work ethic is now outdated and success means thinking about what you desire in every area of your life. You can indulge in that hobby, whatever it is, just for the fun of it, because it really is essential for managing stress.

Preparing for anything you know will be stressful requires effort and even discipline, but the pay-off is huge. Competence gives you confidence so your stress diminishes. The more prepared you are the more you'll find you can approach different situations, enabling you to flourish – an essential part of real calm.

We encourage you to try meditation as this has ample proven benefits. Many people swear by it and others don't take to it. The only way to know is to try it, ideally with a teacher you like. Finally there is exercise and ideally this will double up as something you want to do more of because it gives you joy. Whether you choose Zumba dance classes, a gym workout, running or walking, exercise not only benefits your body, it benefits your moods.

"Instead of getting drunk, I went on a mindfulness course" *– John*

'I've always been Jack the Lad, proud of my hedonistic lifestyle. But it was slowly niggling me that I felt suffocated in relationships and didn't want to be tied to one woman – only when I was on my own I felt lonely and anxious. I couldn't understand this anxiety. It was a horrible feeling so I just drank to get rid of it.

As my mates began to settle, there was no avoiding this. I didn't have mates on tap to go out drinking, and with more and more work responsibility and pressures, hooking up with women for the night became impractical. I couldn't go into work in yesterday's shirt and I start work before shops open to buy a new shirt. There comes a point when certain behaviour isn't cool and funny. When you're leading a team you are setting an example. I could feel that as I got older I wasn't so chilled as I liked to claim. I'd snap and get angry – and then feel guilty and make up for it by offering to buy drinks later.

I realized I was drinking more on my own in the evenings, and the mornings became about psyching myself up to going into work and putting on a front. Only I was always in a flap, easily irritable and increasingly stressed about work pressures. Every couple of months I'd have the euphoria of a new love affair, then I'd run away or be unfaithful and the cycle started again.

I guess I was in the right place to say yes to going on a mindfulness weekend course with a mate suffering from severe stress. His job was on the line and he was going through a messy divorce with two toddlers in between. I suggested a weekend in Prague getting drunk, but he said he needed to try out mindfulness. I thought: 'well I could always skive off to the pub if it is rubbish'.

That was a couple of years ago and I have practised mindfulness since, going on several courses. I realized that first weekend that for all my Jack the Lad image that I projected, I'd always had a side to me connected to something else – the running in nature, the exercise with the guys in the gym, eating well, giving myself time every day to think clearly. It was like the pre-training to mindfulness and realizing this made me aware of the situations where I did feel calm. Calm to me means being able to handle anything coming at me. What I couldn't handle was my own negative feelings. I had to learn not to stuff them with alcohol and release stress by shouting at people.

I am a work in progress. I'm back on top at work and supporting my team and fellow managers and talking openly about how we all feel stressed and sharing ways to ease this like playing silly games. I make time for my family – my parents, my brother and his wife and children. I haven't cracked relationships yet but I'm learning about what I really need.'

ASK YOURSELF

Q How can you develop new supportive connections with people? Can you build on existing friendships – can you nurture these? Or do you need new people in your life?

Q What hobby or activity have you always wanted to take up but never had time for?

Q What would you like to do more of?

Q Which outdoor activities did you like as a child? Which sports did you enjoy as a child?

CHAPTER 10

KEEP CALM
AND CARRY ON
EVERY DAY

he expression 'Keep Calm and Carry On' was coined by the Government's Ministry of Information in 1939 for one of the posters intended to boost the public morale for World War II. But this particular poster was never used.[1] The print run was pulped except for a few. One poster was discovered in 2000 by a bookseller, and another 15 by the BBC Antiques Road Show[2] in 2012. The fact that it has become such a successful commercial enterprise shows how it chimed a chord with our frantic and uncertain modern life.

You will remember from Chapter 6 that we identified six stress triggers that you need to be aware of as they are easy traps to fall into, leading to the frustration of never making it to your calm state. In Chapter 9 we gave you six specific processes to boost calmness in your life.

To be able to choose the skill of calm you have to also cultivate a calm lifestyle. Through living a life that boosts your calm energy at every level you will find yourself able to ramp up your competitive streak and slow down totally to rest, you'll be able to methodically deal with meteoric life problems while still being able to enjoy a hobby, you'll be able to passionately protect yourself and others when under attack without feeling totally wiped out. That's what this final chapter is for.

In fact, rather than the need to Keep Calm and Carry On every day, we suggest carrying on (calmly) every day to keep calm. In this chapter we show you how.

HAVE A HEALTH MAKE OVER

In Chapter 2, one of the major reasons we presented for needing to be calm is health. If we don't manage stress our health is affected, and if our health is affected we're less able to manage stress.

Speaking to your GP about how stress affects you is a good starting point. Tests like cholesterol, vitamin D and thyroid function can shed light on how your body is responding so that you have a clear idea of what to focus on, and if necessary seek additional advice. Even if you are diagnosed with something seemingly unrelated to stress, it's worth bearing in mind that some conditions, notably IBS, are linked to stress. GPs don't necessarily have all the solutions, but any diagnosis is a good starting point for you to take control of your mind and body and investigate further.

If you're a smoker, the single biggest action you can take towards calmness is to seek support to stop smoking. In 2004, University of Michigan scientists[3] found compelling new evidence that smoking alters the way 'feel good' chemicals move between brain cells.

If smoking, alcohol, drugs and junk food are your way of coping with stress, then even acknowledging this is a start (rather than insisting this is how you have fun and you can handle 'it'). Many local authorities have units for specialist support or you can seek help privately, but we recommend first seeing your GP for advice.

GET STRATEGIC ABOUT YOUR DAY

Once you've got major health issues tackled, you can look to managing your responses every day. Every day you know you have a certain routine which typically consists of getting up, commuting to work and back. In addition (or instead) you may have family commitments, you might also be studying or creating something new (whether that's a new business or writing thrillers). Planning how all the areas of your life will coexist will help you manage your time and stay calm, instead of running around trying to keep up with yourself. Calm is all in the detail. Would you rather queue for 20 minutes to buy your lunch so that by the time you arrive back at the office there's not much time left and you gobble it down? Or can you bring last night's leftovers and sit on a bench by the fountain?

Save your calm energy reserves.

- 'First thing in the morning, when you brush your teeth, think of three things you are grateful for. This trains your mind to notice what's good about your life and sets you up for a positive day – instead of anticipating a stressful, bad day.

- Ground yourself with some physical activity before you go to work. This helps you avoid getting caught up in looping thoughts. If you work from home, go for a walk in the local park. If you take public transport, have a good walk to the station or part of the way. Doing something physical helps put you into a positive frame of mind so you start your day in a calm way.

- If you're on public transport, mentally scan each part of your body. This grounds you and helps you tune in to your body instead of getting caught up in anxious thoughts.

- Have plants around you in the office so that you can breathe the oxygen they produce.

- The brain can't concentrate for more than 20 minutes, so try to take regular breaks. Splashing cold water on your face helps to stimulate the vagus nerve which is refreshing and is a quick way to feel relaxed.

- Social media can be positive in that it creates a sense of community, but if it's a permanent distraction it's not helping. Find healthy distractions.'

"You're not in charge of trains so work on accepting that there is little you can do about delays and cancellations instead of getting stuck in anger."

Ed Halliwell, mindfulness teacher and writer

SANDRA ELSDON VIGON ON MAKING CONSCIOUS DECISIONS ABOUT YOUR DAY

'Making conscious decisions is the key – if I watch the news at ten and then wonder why I can't sleep, I can make a change and try not watching the news.

To make practical lifestyle changes our attitude has to be that there is always more than one way, rather than getting stuck in any one particular way. We have to constantly ask: what do I need to do to take care of myself? Where am I empty? Where do I need filling up? There are many ways and it's a matter of finding what works for you.

One of the biggest lessons I've learnt as I grow older is that we need to be able to adapt. Being flexible enables us to adapt to the twists and turns of life. There's nothing you can do about a traffic warden giving you a parking ticket because you're late. Accept and let go. Once you become flexible and adaptable you begin to question how you use your energy, because every action and reaction we have uses up energy. You begin to process things in a different way. You have a choice to waste energy over the traffic warden or channel that energy into something that gives you joy instead.'

GO TO THE PARK AND MOVE

In Chapter 9 we identified exercise as a key way to boost calm and we had plenty of evidence on why exercise helps the brain function. Exercising outside adds to the benefits. A report in 2010[4] based on ten UK studies found that just five minutes of exercise outdoors in nature is good for mental health and wellbeing. This was the first time scientists pinpointed a specific time. Any form of exercise we can do outdoors gives our brains a huge mood boost, according to extensive research at the University of Essex.[5] The university's department – Green Exercise – is continually researching the benefits.

Being in nature is officially and scientifically calming, whether that's a spot of gardening or a full blown run. If you're near water too there's an added bonus. There's no need to fret if you live in a city and getting to the countryside isn't feasible, as the research shows the benefits apply to exercise in urban parks.

PROFESSOR ROBERTSON ON SUPER SIMPLE TIPS TO CHANGE OUR BRAIN CHEMISTRY AT ANY TIME

'We have an amazing ability to change our brain chemistry – which changes our emotions. There are so many simple ways to do this.

- *Breathe!*
- *Take a brisk walk round the park.*
- *Change your routine – do something a little bit different.*
- *Don't read the news or look at Facebook while eating a sandwich. Enjoy the sandwich.*
- *During any difficult conversation take a full breath before replying. Remind yourself to speak in a lower voice so you are breathing properly.'*

ASK YOURSELF

I can kickstart my calm day by ...

One thing I can change to make my work day better is ...

The triggers I need to avoid are ...

To get some physical exercise I can ...

What always makes me smile is ... so I'm going to make sure I ...

CHOOSE CAREFULLY WHAT YOUR MIND CONSUMES

Everything we put into our mind is a form of food, if you like. And in our modern culture we are constantly filling our minds. We're privileged to be able to access so much information, to enjoy entertainment without even leaving home, and to easily connect with others. But we know and you know that there's a flip side to this.

Our modern life is saturated with stimulation, from TV to social media. You might very well find yourself with the TV on, checking your messages on your smartphone, looking something up on your tablet – and cross referencing with your laptop, while downloading something on your kindle and yet something else on your computer. As you know now from Chapter 6, a major stress trigger is a wandering mind. To cultivate calm you need to cultivate sustained attention.

There are other reasons too to consider what your mind consumes. If your way of escaping is to play computer games, for example, how does this nourish you? Brad Bushman, professor of communication and psychology at Ohio State University, has carried out several studies on the damaging effects of violent games. But in one study[6] he found that *relaxing* video games can have a positive effect on mood.

Passive activities like watching TV can amount to zoning out and, of course, as Jungian psychotherapist Sandra Elsdon Vigon agrees, there are times we need to do this. However, there's a big difference between consciously zoning out for a short while and unconsciously zoning out for hours.

Psychologist and neuroscientist, Professor Robertson, points to ample evidence of TV sapping our mental energy. What our brains need is 'brain fertilizer' – and that comes from other activities like education and learning something new.[7] These activities also keep our minds young.

ED HALLIWELL ON SMARTPHONES, SOCIAL MEDIA AND NEWS

'Most people start their morning by turning on their phones, looking at news and emails. This sets up the day for anxiety.

The difficulty with news is that it's all of the bad news so it's biased. There are lots of pleasant things which don't get reported so we get a particular filter through the media. The media is made of human beings and human beings are more alert to threats than pleasant experiences, because we are trying to survive. This then reinforces our own bias, so we are looking out for threat all the time. Our minds are naturally inclined towards what is difficult and threatening. We may well want to be engaged in the world, but it's important to recognize that this is a biased interpretation.

Then it's about choosing when to consume the news. Consuming news can give us a sense of powerlessness; if we can't do anything or help in some way we're overwhelmed. If all we are doing is consuming news we not helping the world.

With social media, the message that we often receive is everybody else is happier than me, so it's the other way round. People present a version of wonderful and we feel inadequate. We can be aware of these biases and the fragmentation of attention that comes from constantly looking.

We could ask ourselves: How can I be in wise relationships to news and social media? It's about making decisions like: I will read my newspaper app once a day instead of 20 times. I need to trust I will get enough to be connected to the world. Similarly with email and Twitter.

We can turn great ways of connecting very easily into obsessions. We take the wonderful capacity to be in touch with the world and twist it. This can then create more self-criticism. Everything feeds in and affects our mind and body, so we need to take care of what our minds consume, especially as we are often ingesting a biased view of the world.'

GO CALM FROM THE INSIDE OUT: EAT TO BOOST YOUR MIND AND MOOD

There's a lot of exciting recent research still in early stages about the relationship between the gut and the brain and how our moods are affected. We do know for sure that there are significant links. Many of the neurotransmitters (chemical messengers) that make us feel better, like serotonin and GABA, are made in the gut.

One recent study[8] explored whether bacteria in the gut can be used to cure or prevent stress, anxiety and depression. Much of this research is focused on helping people recovering from post-traumatic stress disorder (PTSD), but there are relevant implications for all of us. The microbes in our intestinal tract influence our food digestion, immune system and send signals to the brain affecting mood.

When it comes to eating to be calm, it's not just about what you eat, but how. Ensure you take time to do the food justice. Nutritional therapist Eve Kalinik, our nutrition columnist, provides some tips. Her forthcoming book, *Eat Well,* has more advice.[9]

EVE KALINIK ON LOOKING AFTER YOUR GUT SO THAT IT LOOKS AFTER YOU

'The gut is a major part of the nervous system, so when you're stressed the gut responds in different ways. This can be through gut motility (rapid movements or total no-go), reduced gastric juice secretion which impairs breaking down food (bloating) and an impairing of the gut barrier (affecting absorption of nutrients). Weight gain can also be a stress side effect because of the gut not working optimally.

Chronic stress can alter the microorganisms in the gut, reducing microbial diversity and beneficial bacteria that are important to gut health. Stress can lead to a variety of gut disorders like the ubiquitous IBS and other digestive conditions such as IBD, reflux (GERD) and peptic ulcers. (A stool test will reveal the state of your gut and its microorganisms, as well as how your digestive system is working.)

Here's some advice to remember every day:

- *We should be using the bedroom for two things and checking emails is not one of them. When the first thing you do is check your emails from your bed you are putting your body into fight or flight mode. Stay in rest and digest mode when you wake up.*

- *Avoid coffee on an empty stomach (and in excess throughout the day).*

- *Most of my clients eat their lunch at their desk. I encourage them to at least take their mind away from work and social media by using a calming screen saver (green is a good colour for this), to chew properly, taking 20 minutes ideally to finish.*

- *It's important to understand that the body cannot be in two places at the same time. It cannot be in rest and digest mode while it's in fight or flight stress-survival mode. Stressed eating keeps us discombobulated. We need to be present and aware when eating. Being present with our plate and using meal times as pockets of recovery can accumulatively have such a profound effect. I recommend reading* How to Eat *by Thich-Nhat-Hanh.*

- *For most people, cooked food is easier to digest than raw food, so during stress periods aim for more soups and aim to take in raw food earlier in the day.*

- *Look after your gut by eating plenty of the fermented foods like sauerkraut, kefir, kimchi, pickles and kombucha, as well as sourdough bread. Wild salmon and also grass-fed organic meat provide good sources of omega 3 which is important to support anti-inflammatory processes. Eat vegetables in abundance. Around two brazil nuts will give your RDI for selenium, which is one of the micronutrients that we tend to lack.*

Introduce a daily probiotic as this is important for gut health and supports the reduction of stress internally. (Scientists at University College Hospital have found that Symprove[10] is effective.)

Avoid excessive alcohol.

It doesn't matter how well you eat, how much exercise you do or the multitude of supplements you knock back, stress will sabotage all of your best efforts. Having pockets of recovery on a daily basis are essential for wellbeing and health.'

Everyone loves the reclaimed war time motto 'Keep Calm and Carry On'. As you can see, the process is really 'carry on with stress management every day throughout the day' in order to keep calm. Paying attention to every detail in your life is rather like decluttering and tidying up your entire home including your wardrobe.

Taking an in-depth look at where you're at medically, and giving yourself a health make over if necessary, will put you in a prime position to manage stress. Instead of giving in to the demands of daily life, you can take control of every aspect of your day and seek out practical ways to help yourself throughout the day – from handling days in the office to how you choose to spend your evenings. Formulating a strategy to deal with your working day will help you manage the pressures. Paying special attention to what your mind consumes can not only help you focus on being calm, it can also ensure you're not sabotaging your efforts to manage stress. Considering how you use your smartphone might be one of the most important changes you make.

We hope this book has demystified how the brain works and that you are reassured that there are some very simple and scientifically proven ways to change your brain's chemistry. One of the simplest is going for a brisk walk in the park. You can help to boost your mind by avoiding stimulants like coffee and alcohol, and eating healthily so that your body is nourished and armed with the nutrients you need to sustain the right amount of stress. Finally, it's essential to look after your gut since the latest research is pointing to huge links between the gut and the brain.

Lifestyle isn't about fancy photos on Instagram, glossy brochures and the fantasy lives of others. Lifestyle is the style in which you live your daily life and we hope you will be inspired to live in the style of calm.

ASK YOURSELF

Q I'm going to try out ...

Q Instead of just flopping in front of the TV I'll also ...

Q Instead of just crashing out at the weekends with a box set I will also ...

Q I can improve my diet by cutting down ... and eating more ...

WHAT NEXT?

Now that you've reached the end of this book, you will be in a much stronger position to handle stress because you have an understanding of what happens in your mind and body and how the link between the two affects your thoughts and feelings. There's a lot of information in this little book, so you might like to re-read sections that apply to you, as well as the advice that appeals to you.

You know having read this far that there are no quick fixes, but there are plenty of ways available to handle stress. Now is the time to explore these different methods and to find what process leads you to feeling calm, able to handle the challenges of life and to enjoy life too. We've given you a lot to think about in terms of why and how you get into a state in the first place – and we don't want you to forget that changing this into a calm state is more about *doing* something rather than thinking your way out of it.

We hope that the key messages have resonated with you: that feeling calm isn't about being permanently laid back, that once you understand how much stress your body can handle you can protect yourself from excess stress, and that it's possible to even thrive on stress.

Of course we hope that, having come this far, you will feel optimistic about developing the skills to be calm in difficult situations and so you'll go back to this book again and again. You might even enjoy the process a tiny bit, dare we say, you may even get excited. Before you sat down to read this book you might never have imagined that stress can be rebranded into excitement, that you can rev it up in a good way to go on a fabulous journey rather than allowing it drive you to a crash.

We've provided you with the tools to be your own stress manager and to develop a system to find moments of calm in your life. Through our coaching questions and tests you can discover which situations derail you and trigger you. We've included the latest scientific research so that you know why it's medically important to get a handle on stress, and which methods of doing so really are effective. Through our panel of six leading experts you have a multi-dimensional view on the umbrella that is stress.

However you choose to use this book from now on, one thing is definite. If you want to be calm, it's a wish and a need you have to commit to on a daily basis. However you do that is up to you, and we hope you will embrace some or many of the suggestions. But remember not to allow yourself from now on to spiral into a negative state that's so deep that climbing out of it is a wrench. It's better to make one tiny change at a time, every day, than attempt a major change every few months that isn't sustainable. (Hello New Year's Resolutions – or rather goodbye.)

We wish you all the best calm moments every day in as many ways that you can find them. A calm life is an engaged and excited life, because calmness gives you the energy to live your life the way you want to.

ABOUT PSYCHOLOGIES

Psychologies is a magazine read by those who want to lead a fulfilling life, who want to live a life on their own terms, however you choose to define it. *Psychologies* helps you discover what 'life success' looks like for you – from the inside out.

We're on a mission to find out from the best experts and the latest research in psychology how we can all lead happier and more fulfilling lives. Psychologies is not about striving to do more but rather finding ways to BE more. Who are you? And what do you really want? These are questions we're always asking ourselves. *Psychologies* magazine is about being the best you, and we mean being in an active way: becoming the best you can be, the happiest and the most fulfilled you.

We focus on helping you understand yourself and the world around you, by gathering the latest, most compelling thinking and translating it into practical wisdom that can support you as you create the life that works for you.

Real Calm is written by Lorna V, who also wrote the first book in our series, *Real Confidence,* and the third *Real Ambition*. Lorna graduated from the London School of Economics and then followed her dream to be a journalist, working for national newspapers and magazines. She has written widely about lifestyle, wellbeing, complementary health and psychology – putting what she has learnt along the way into practice. Her first play was shortlisted for the Verity Bargate theatre award and she was invited onto the Soho Theatre One Year Writers' Attachment Programme. She recently embarked on performing her own work as an actor.

www.LornaV.com   @LornaVwriter

REFERENCES

INTRODUCTION

1. www.dailymail.co.uk/health/article-3727507/Teenagers-stress-anxiety-levels-time-high-middle-class-children-worst-affected.html
2. www.anxietyuk.org.uk/our-services/anxiety-information/frequently-asked-questions/
3. www.hse.gov.uk/statistics/causdis/stress/
4. www.adaa.org/about-adaa/press-room/facts-statistics
5. www.npr.org/sections/health-shots/2014/07/07/323351759/for-many-americans-stress-takes-a-toll-on-health-and-family

CHAPTER 1

1. www.etymonline.com/index.php?term=calm
2. http://buddhify.com
3. www.spire.io
4. http://journal.frontiersin.org/article/10.3389/fnagi.2016.00098/full
5. Ian Robertson (2016) *The Stress Test: How Pressure Can Make You Stronger and Sharper* (Bloomsbury), p. 55; S. L. Beilock (2008) 'Math performance in stressful situations.' *Current Directions in Psychological Science* 17(5) 339–43.
6. R. M. Yerkes and J. D. Dodson (1908) 'The relation of strength of stimulous to rapidity of habit-formation.' *Journal of Comparative and Neurological Psychology* 18, 459–82.

CHAPTER 2

1. Roy F. Baumeister and John Tierney (2012) *Willpower: Rediscovering Our Greatest Strength* (Penguin).
2. *Psychologies* magazine February 2012.

3. Mihály Csíkszentmihályi (2000) *Beyond Boredom and Anxiety: Experiencing Flow in Work and Play* (Wiley).

4. Carnegie Mellon University 'How stress influences disease: Study reveals inflammation as the culprit.' *ScienceDaily*, 2 April 2012. www.sciencedaily.com/releases/2012/04/120402162546.htm

5. Penn State 'Keep calm and carry on, for the sake of your long-term health.' *ScienceDaily*, 9 June 2015. www.sciencedaily.com/releases/2015/06/150609121952.htm

6. University of Sydney 'Keep calm, anger can trigger a heart attack!' *ScienceDaily*, 24 February 2015. www.sciencedaily.com/releases/2015/02/150224083819.htm

7. American College of Cardiology 'Over time, those who find inner calm live longer, healthier lives.' *ScienceDaily*, 15 May 2007. www.sciencedaily.com/releases/2007/05/070514174254.htm

8. B. B.Schiff and M. Lamon (1994) 'Inducing emotion by unilateral contraction of hand muscles.' *Cortex* 30(2) 247–54.

9. www.ted.com/speakers/amy_cuddy

10. www1.lehigh.edu/news/after-hours-email-expectations-hurt-employee-well-being

11. University of Toronto, Rotman School of Management 'Calm candidates perform better on tests used to screen job applicants.' *ScienceDaily,* 4 November 2013. www.sciencedaily.com/releases/2013/11/131104123742.htm

12. Ed Halliwell (2016) *Into the Heart of Mindfulness* (Piatkus), p. 4.

13. University of Wisconsin-Madison 'For comfort, mom's voice works as well as a hug.' *ScienceDaily*, 12 May 2010. www.sciencedaily.com/releases/2010/05/100511201730.htm

14. Louisiana State University Health Sciences Center 'Emotional stress can change brain function.' *ScienceDaily*, 12 January 2011. www.sciencedaily.com/releases/2011/01/110112132409.htm

CHAPTER 3

1. www.drweil.com/drw/u/VDR00112/The-4-7-8-Breath-Benefits-and-Demonstration.html

2. www.drweil.com/drw/u/ART00521/three-breathing-exercises.html

CHAPTER 4

1. www.simplypsychology.org/bowlby.html
2. Ian Robertson (2016) *The Stress Test: How Pressure Can Make You Stronger And Sharper* (Bloomsbury) p. 12
3. J. A. Rob Gray (1990) 'Brain Systems that mediate both emotion and cognition.' *Cognition & Emotion* 4(3) 269–88.
4. R. J. Davidson (1992) 'Anterior cerebral asymmetry and the nature of emotion.' *Brain and Cognition*, 20(1) 125–51.
5. http://worldhappiness.report/ed/2016/
6. Meik Wiking (2016) *The Little Book of Hygge: The Danish Way to Live Well* (Penguin Life).
7. Jim Loehr and Tony Schwartz (2005) *The Power of Full Engagement: Managing Energy, not Time, is the Key to High Performance and Personal Renewal* (Simon & Schuster).
8. Ian Robertson (2016) *The Stress Test: How Pressure Can Make You Stronger And Sharper* (Bloomsbury), p. 137.
9. Ibid. p. 147.
10. Ibid. p. 200.

CHAPTER 5

1. www.nhs.uk/Tools/Pages/Mood-self-assessment.aspx
2. Mount Sinai Health System 'Systems biology research study reveals benefits of vacation, meditation'. *ScienceDaily*, 30 August 2016. www.sciencedaily.com/releases/2016/08/160830091815.htm
3. Baycrest Centre for Geriatric Care 'Chronic stress, anxiety can damage the brain, increase risk of major psychiatric disorders.' *ScienceDaily*, 21 January 2016. www.sciencedaily.com/releases/2016/01/160121121818.htm

CHAPTER 6

1. Ian Robertson (2016) *The Stress Test: How Pressure Can Make You Stronger And Sharper* (Bloomsbury), p. 39.

2. M. A. Killingsworth and D. T. Gilbert (2010) 'A wandering mind is an unhappy mind.' *Science*, 330(6006), 932.
3. Ian Robertson (2016) *The Stress Test: How Pressure Can Make You Stronger And Sharper* (Bloomsbury), p. 63.
4. www.mindsetonline.com

CHAPTER 7

1. Rockefeller University 'Newly discovered windows of brain plasticity may help stress-related disorders.' *ScienceDaily*, 23 December 2015. www.sciencedaily.com/releases/2015/12/151223141338.htm
2. Ian Robertson (2016) *The Stress Test: How Pressure Can Make You Stronger And Sharper* (Bloomsbury), p. 14.

CHAPTER 8

1. Reneau Z. Peurifoy (2010) *Anxiety Phobias and Panic* (Piatkus), p. 73.
2. Ibid. p. 65.
3. Ian Robertson (2016) *The Stress Test: How Pressure Can Make You Stronger And Sharper* (Bloomsbury), p. 122.
4. American Psychological Association 'Getting excited helps with performance anxiety more than trying to calm down, study finds.' *ScienceDaily*, 23 December 2013. www.sciencedaily.com/releases/2013/12/131223083917.htm

CHAPTER 9

1. www.vitalfriends.com. Tom Rath (2006) *Vital Friends: The People You Can't Afford to Live Without*. (Gallup Press).
2. http://webuser.bus.umich.edu/janedut/
3. www.positivityratio.com
4. www.dailymail.co.uk/femail/article-3643816/RAGE-ERCISE-fitness-class-sweeping-country-women-yell-write-angry-thoughts-balloons-popping-them.html
5. www.tantrumclub.com

6. Ian Robertson (2016) *The Stress Test: How Pressure Can Make You Stronger And Sharper* (Bloomsbury), p. 176.

7. The Norwegian University of Science and Technology (NTNU) 'This is your brain on meditation: Brain processes more thoughts, feelings during meditation, study shows.' *ScienceDaily*, 15 May 2014. www.sciencedaily.com/releases/2014/05/140515095545.htm

8. University of Washington 'Mindful multitasking: Meditation first can calm stress, aid concentration.' *ScienceDaily*, 14 June 2012. www.sciencedaily.com/releases/2012/06/120614094118.htm

9. British Psychological Society (BPS) 'Online mindfulness intervention reduces fatigue, negative work-related worry.' *ScienceDaily*, 9 September 2014. www.sciencedaily.com/releases/2014/09/140909191959.htm

10. University of Maryland 'Exercise may protect against future emotional stress, study shows.' *ScienceDaily*, 13 September 2012. www.sciencedaily.com/releases/2012/09/120913123629.htm

11. University of California – Davis Health System 'This is your brain on exercise: Vigorous exercise boosts critical neurotransmitters, may help restore mental health.' *ScienceDaily*, 25 February 2016. www.sciencedaily.com/releases/2016/02/160225101241.htm

CHAPTER 10

1. www.keepcalmandcarryon.com/history

2. www.dailymail.co.uk/news/article-2105518/Keep-calm-carry-Only-surviving-stash-original-iconic-poster-appears-Antiques-Roadshow.html#ixzz1oMO2BFNH

3. University Of Michigan Health System 'First evidence that smoking affects brain's natural "feel good" chemical system.' *ScienceDaily*, 28 October 2004. www.sciencedaily.com/releases/2004/10/041027141507.htm

4. American Chemical Society 'In the green of health: Just 5 minutes of "green exercise" optimal for good mental health.' *ScienceDaily*, 21 May 2010. www.sciencedaily.com/releases/2010/05/100502080414.htm

REFERENCES

5. www.greenexercise.org/menu
6. *Ohio State University* 'Kinder, gentler video games may actually be good for players.' *ScienceDaily*, 6 June 2011. www.sciencedaily.com/releases/2011/06/110606113403.htm
7. Ian Robertson (2016) *The Stress Test: How Pressure Can Make You Stronger And Sharper* (Bloomsbury), p. 171.
8. Office of Naval Research 'Gut feeling: Research examines link between stomach bacteria, PTSD.' *ScienceDaily*, 25 April 2016. www.sciencedaily.com/releases/2016/04/160425161324.htm
9. www.evekalinik.com, @EveKalinik, Eve's book, *Eat Well: How to Have a Healthier, Happier Gut* (Piatkus) is out in September 2017.
10. www.symprove.com

Notes

Notes